The Problem of
Altruism

The Problem of Altruism

Freudian–Darwinian Solutions

C. R. BADCOCK

Basil Blackwell

Basil Blackwell Ltd
108 Cowley Road, Oxford OX4 1JF, UK

Basil Blackwell Inc.
432 Park Avenue South, Suite 1503,
New York, NY 10016, USA

British Library Cataloguing in Publication Data

Badcock, C.R.
The problem of altruism.
1. Sociobiology   2. Altruism
I. Title
304.5   GN365.9
ISBN 0-631-13814-5

Library of Congress Cataloging in Publication Data

Badcock, C. R.
The problem of altruism.

Bibliography: p.
Includes index.
1. Altruism.   2. Altruistic behavior in animals.
3. Freud, Sigmund, 1856–1939 — Views of altruism.
I. Title.
BF637.H4B32 1986   155.2'32   86–1112

ISBN 0-631-13814-5

Typeset by Katerprint Company Limited, Oxford, England
Printed in Great Britain by Bell and Bain Ltd, Glasgow

Contents

Acknowledgements

I would like to thank David Barash, Rose and Milton Friedman, William Hamilton, Keith Hopkins, Mancur Olson, and especially Robert Trivers for permission to quote from their works. I must also thank my colleagues, Jean Aitchison, Percy Cohen, Roger Holmes, Donald MacRae and David McKnight for their helpful comments on the manuscript, and Alma Gibbons in particular and the LSE computer department staff in general for their patient and generous help with the preparation of the text. Finally, I owe a very special debt of gratitude to John Davey of Basil Blackwell for his untiring and loyal support, advice and guidance at every stage of the composition of the book. The views expressed in it are, of course, entirely my own.

C. R. Badcock
September 1985

Introduction:
As with Darwin, so with Freud . . .

Revolution and reaction in science

Today everyone knows that Sigmund Freud regarded psychoanalysis as a major scientific revolution but, equally, today everyone knows that he was wrong. Now, almost a century after the psychoanalytic revolution may be regarded as having begun, few who would readily ascribe a revolutionary status to the discovery of the heliocentric solar system or evolution by natural selection would also ascribe it to the discovery of the unconscious. Today everyone knows that even many of Freud's own followers could not be convinced of the correctness of his views and that early defections by Adler, Jung and numerous others have been followed by a bewildering profusion of divergent psychoanalytic and psychotherapeutic schools, each claiming a monopoly of the truth. Some – even more damaging to the scientific pretensions of psychoanalysis – have long since given up the claim to be scientific and emphasize a subjectivism which bears out all that the self-appointed guardians of science have long been saying: psychoanalysis is 'unscientific', breaks all the canons of proper scientific method and has been disproved or, at the very least, cannot be proved by any reputable scientific means.

It would seem that the best one could do for Freud in this respect is to picture him as some latter-day Leeuwenhoek, and his psychoanalytic method as the psychological equivalent of the seventeenth-century microscopist's instruments.

These were the best part of two centuries ahead of their time and revealed a world so far removed from everyday experience and so weird in appearance that its discoverer inevitably became the butt of satirists and of fellow scientists whose inability to corroborate his findings was bound to leave him isolated, misunderstood and generally discredited until rescued from obscurity and derision by later scientific advances. 'Those who know how to wait,' Freud once remarked, 'need make no concessions.'[1]

Yet those who subscribe to this, or even to a more negative view of psychoanalysis, would do well to ponder a moment on the very examples of successful and accepted scientific revolutions which they might be tempted to hold up for comparison with it. It is worth remarking that, just as psychoanalysis is written off by many today, so 'In the early years of the twentieth century Darwinism was considered moribund', and that 'For the first forty or fifty years of Darwin's theory of evolution . . . the evidence of both physics and biology were against Darwin's original theory':[2]

> At the turn of the century, the fortunes of evolutionary theory had reached their lowest ebb. Physicists to a man had proved that the earth was not nearly as old as Darwin's theory required. Geneticists such as de Vries and Morgan were claiming that mutations were discrete, not gradual; thus, Darwin had been wrong in thinking that evolution was gradual. The excesses of evolutionists like Haeckel and the disputes concerning orthogenesis and neo-Lamarckianism had earned for evolution a decidedly bad reputation. It was more metaphysics than science.[3]

Then-fashionable philosophies of science held that Darwin's arguments could be dismissed as 'mere analogies', much as those of Freud were to be later or those of Copernicus had

[1] S. Freud, *Group Psychology and the Analysis of the Ego*, XVIII, 91. This and any subsequent reference to the works of Sigmund Freud is to the Standard Edition of the *Complete Psychological Works of Sigmund Freud*, quoting volume and page number.

[2] L. Ritvo, 'Darwin as the Origin of Freud's Neo-Lamarckianism', *Journal of the American Psychoanalytic Association*, 13, 1965, pp. 504 and 505.

[3] D. Hull, *Darwin and his Critics*, p. 34.

been earlier. Evolutionary theory as a whole was held to be quite unacceptable, in part because it was non-teleological (i.e., did not argue from design, but assumed random mutations).[4] Today, of course, everyone knows that teleology is a hall-mark of *un*scientific method – an example which shows just how much views on such issues can change in relatively short periods of time.

Unlike Freud who wanted to avoid making 'concessions to faintheartedness',[5] Darwin evidently did not see the virtues of waiting for final vindication and certainly seems to have been ready to make considerable concessions to contemporary critics of his theory:

> No sooner had he published the *Origin of Species* than Darwin began to undo what he had accomplished. Only the first edition of the *Origin of Species* is relatively free from Darwin's ambivalence towards his theory. In all subsequent editions of the *Origin* as well as in his succeeding works . . . Darwin protested more and more that he really had not meant it.[6]

Indeed, so apparent did this become with time and with succeeding editions that a modern biologist has suggested that by the sixth the title should have read: *On the Origin of Species by Means of Natural Selection and All Sorts of Other Things*[7] including, evidently, a liberal dose of that Neo-Lamarckianism which nowadays is usually regarded as the exact antithesis of his theory.

If Darwin was ambivalent about his Darwinism, one might well wonder whether Copernicus was not equally ambivalent about his Copernicanism. In support of this view one might cite his delay in publishing the work propounding his new theory until he was on his death-bed, not to mention devoting so much of it to elaborating the old Ptolemaic

---

[4] Ibid., p. 60. This evaluation was the view of no less a philosopher than J. S. Mill.

[5] S. Freud, *Group Psychology*, XVIII, 91.

[6] Ritvo, 'Darwin', p. 504.

[7] R. M. Young, quoted by R. Dawkins, *The Extended Phenotype*, p. 19.

system. Certainly there is no doubt that we would be quite
wrong to imagine that his idea was immediately, or even
quickly, accepted. According to an authoritative account, the
success of Copernicus' book

> does not imply the success of its central thesis. The faith of
> most astronomers in the earth's stability was at first
> unshaken. Authors who applauded Copernicus' erudition,
> borrowed his diagrams, or quoted his determination of the
> distance from the earth to the moon, usually either ignored
> the earth's motion or dismissed it as absurd. Even the rare
> text that mentioned Copernicus' hypothesis with respect
> rarely defended or used it.[8]

As the author of this quotation has commented, 'It is easy to
understand the existence of strong resistance to Copernicus'
revolution – its patent absurdity and destructiveness were not
offset by effective evidence.'[9] He adds that even sixty-seven
years later, when Galileo first turned a telescope on the
heavens, one could only say that it 'argued much, it proved
nothing.'[10]

Despite the efforts of the founder of modern astronomy,
the model of the solar system which first became established
after Copernicus' death was not his but that of Tycho Brahe.
It was a system which accommodated part of Copernicus'
radical new idea by having all the other planets in orbit round
the sun but which restored the earth to the unmoving centre
of the universe and had the sun circling the earth just as it did
in the old Ptolemaic system. It was, in short, a botched and
bungled compromise, one which is reminiscent of Darwin's
later and much modified evolutionary theory and one which
may also come to be seen as a parallel with modern Neo-
Freudianism and much of present-day psychoanalysis in
general. Such examples as these recall Einstein's remark that

[8] T. S. Kuhn, *The Copernican Revolution*, p. 186.
[9] Ibid., p. 195.
[10] Ibid., p. 226.

'Scientific greatness is essentially a matter of character. The main thing is to refuse to make rotten compromises.'[11]

Yet, however much the great characters of science may exemplify Einstein's judgement – and, in Freud's case, be roundly condemned for it – rotten compromises usually seem to be the first fruits of great advances in science. Scientific revolutions, evidently, are neither so sudden nor so complete as the term suggests. It appears that they are typified by complexity, confusion and compromise, and generally take much longer to become established than our normal rather casual historical hindsight might suppose. It seems almost incredible that the last published attack on Copernicus should date from 1873 or that the Catholic Church should have kept up its official opposition to Copernicanism until 1822.[12] Today Creationism represents the final stand of religious fundamentalism against evolution, but even within modern Darwinism evidence of confusion and equivocation can still be found. As I shall now attempt to illustrate, where the evolutionary explanation of social behaviour is concerned, a veritable Tychonic compromise came into existence, albeit more or less unintentionally.

Resistance in biological and social science

In recent papers the biologists Robert Trivers and W. D. Hamilton have drawn attention to the fact that even though

> Darwin explicitly realized that natural selection does not favour traits that are good for the species, for the population, or for the group . . . Nevertheless . . . virtually all biologists settled down to the comfortable belief that natural selection favoured what was good for the species.[13]

[11] Quoted in W. Kaufmann, *Discovering the Mind*, vol. III, *Freud versus Adler and Jung*, p. 17.
[12] Ibid., pp. 199 and 227.
[13] R. Trivers, 'Sociobiology and Politics', in E. White (ed.), *Sociobiology and Human Politics*, p. 4.

Trivers adds that 'One can find that view expressed even today within biology, and until the 1960s it was virtually the only view expressed.'[14] Hamilton points out that

> Until the advent of Mendelism uncritical acceptance of group selection could be understood partly on grounds of vagueness about the hereditary process. For example, courage and self-sacrifice could spread by cultural contagion and, in so spreading, modify heredity as well. But in the event neither the rediscovery of Mendel's work nor the fairly brisk incorporation of Mendelism into evolutionary theory had much effect. From about 1920 to about 1960 a curious situation developed where the models of 'Neo-Darwinism' were all concerned with selection at levels no higher than that of competing individuals, whereas the biological literature as a whole increasingly proclaimed faith in Neo-Darwinism, and at the same time stated almost all its interpretations of adaptation in terms of 'benefit to the species'. The leading theorists did occasionally point out the weakness of this position, but on the whole concerned themselves with it surprisingly little.[15]

Speculating on the likely causes of this extraordinary situation, Hamilton expresses the view that

> With facts mostly neutral and theory silent it seems that we must look to the events and the 'isms' of recent human history to understand how such a situation arose. Marxism, trade unionism, fears of 'social Darwinism', and vicissitudes of thought during two world wars seem likely influences. Confronted with common social exhortations, natural selection is easily accused of divisive and reactionary implications unless 'fittest' means the fittest species (man) and 'struggle' means struggle against nature (anything but man). 'Benefit-of-the-species' arguments, so freely used during the period in question, are seen in this light as euphemisms for natural selection. They provide for the reader (and evidently often for the writer as well) escape from inner conflict, exacting

[14] Ibid., p. 4.
[15] W. D. Hamilton, 'Innate Social Aptitudes of Man: An Approach from Evolutionary Genetics', in R. Fox (ed.), *Biosocial Anthropology*, p. 135.

nothing emotionally beyond what most of us learn to accept in childhood, that most forms of life exploit and prey on one another.[16]

Trivers adds that resistance to Darwinism as a whole is explicable in terms of its conflict with traditional religious values. He points out that

> Once it was clear that the pre-Darwinian tradition of species-advantage thinking continued unabated within biology, Christianity as well as other elements in society was able to admit to the *facts* of evolution without risking any of its deeper preconceptions. This must be a common pattern in human history, whereby a concept is transmuted and rendered impotent (natural selection favors what is good for the species) in order to retain older patterns of thought. Thus is progress impeded. Darwin's work became a minor update to the first few pages of Genesis, and nothing more, when in reality Darwin had discovered the exact, ongoing way in which organic creation is achieved.[17]

Hamilton's mention of 'an escape from inner conflict', and Trivers' view that 'a concept is transmuted and rendered impotent in order to retain older patterns of thought' are strikingly similar to what Freud had to say many years before when he catalogued the three principal blows which science had dealt to 'the naïve self-love of men' and suggested that he himself had been responsible for the third:

> The first was when they learnt that our earth was not the centre of the universe but only a tiny fragment of a cosmic system of scarcely imaginable vastness. This is associated in our minds with the name of Copernicus, though something similar had already been asserted by Alexandrian science. The second blow fell when biological research destroyed man's supposedly privileged place in creation and proved his descent from the animal kingdom and his ineradicable animal nature. This revaluation has been accomplished in our own days by Darwin, Wallace and their predecessors, though not without

[16] Ibid., p. 135.
[17] Trivers, 'Sociobiology and Politics', p. 3.

the most violent contemporary opposition. But human megalomania will have suffered its third and most wounding blow from the psychological research of the present time which seeks to prove to the ego that it is not even master in its own house, but must content itself with scanty information of what is going on unconsciously in its mind. We psycho-analysts were not the first and not the only ones to utter this call to introspection; but it seems to be our fate to give it its most forcible expression and to support it with empirical material which affects every individual. Hence arises the general revolt against our science, the disregard of all con-sideration of academic civility and the releasing of the opposi-tion from every restraint of impartial logic.[18]

Auguste Comte, the coiner of the term 'sociology', pro-claimed what he called 'the hierarchy of the sciences'. Science, he alleged, did not advance in all departments equally, but in a logical order, with the more abstract and fundamental sciences preceding the more tangible and speci-fic ones. Hence mathematics was the first of the sciences and achieved its positive, scientific maturity in the ancient world, having evolved out of the metaphysical thinking of the Pythagorians and doubtless earlier and yet more mystical numerologies. Eventually it was followed by physics, which achieved full positive potency with Isaac Newton, and then by chemistry, and then by biology. Such a progression, he thought, was both logical and inevitable.

Nevertheless, the historian of science might well object that if this is a logical and inevitable progression then it is one with some amazingly significant gaps and delays along the way. For, as we have seen Freud observing in the quotation above, Alexandrian science and in particular Aristarchos of Samos had anticipated Copernicus and, although he does not mention it, one might add that Darwin's evolutionary theory had a distinct prefigurement in some of the ideas of Empodocles, Anaximander and Democritus.

Comte probably had a valid point about certain sciences relying on the previous successes of others – as, for instance,

---

[18] S. Freud, *Introductory Lectures on Psychoanalysis*, XVI, pp. 284–5.

physics could be argued to rely on mathematics, and chemistry on physics – yet it nevertheless seems clear that another factor enters into the situation.

An example of what I have in mind might be drawn from early reactions to Darwin's *Origin of Species* within the wider scientific community. Far from being readily accepted as resting on a pre-existing foundation in physical science as Comte might have expected, we encounter a situation in which Lord Kelvin, 'contended by many historians of science to be the outstanding physicist of the nineteenth century',[19] roundly condemned 'the utter futility' of Darwin's theory by thinking that he had proved by purely physical demonstration that the earth was nowhere near old enough for evolutionary changes to have had time to take place.[20] 'Today,' as in Comte's time

> there is a tendency in some quarters to regard the physical sciences as superior in reliability to those in which precise mathematical adeptness has not been achieved. Without wishing to challenge this point of view, it may still be worth a chastening thought that, in this long controversy extending well over half a century, the physicists made extended use of mathematical techniques and still were hopelessly and, it must be added, arrogantly wrong.
>
> By contrast, the geologists who appeared to their physicist colleagues as bumbling amateurs expressing themselves only in vague hunches, and who could produce few arguments that the great Kelvin would deign to notice or to answer, happen to have been remarkably right.[21]

The factor in question (and, almost certainly, the operative motive in Kelvin, who was devoutly religious[22]) is what Freud termed 'resistance'; and we have already seen it invoked by Trivers and Hamilton in order to explain the popularity of group-selectionism and 'good-for-the-species' types of thinking in modern evolutionary biology, not to

[19] L. Eisely, *Darwin's Century*, p. 234.
[20] Ibid., p. 240.
[21] Ibid., p. 234.
[22] Ibid., p. 235.

mention its role in delaying and complicating both the Copernican and original Darwinian revolutions. But it is most unlikely to be an isolated factor, operative only in these specific instances. Far more likely is the probability that analogous needs to escape from 'inner conflict' – Hamilton's words, not Freud's – exist with regard to other sciences, and indeed, that the progress of science as a whole is fundamentally influenced by this phenomenon.

If we had the courage to pursue this idea for a while we might begin to wonder whether Comte's hierarchy was after all not merely the product of inevitable logic but also of human psychology, and that the first sciences were bound to be those furthest away from issues involved most intimately in the 'naïve self-love of men'. Perhaps mathematics comes first in Comte's ordering and appears as the first of the sciences in history because of all sciences it is the most abstract and formal and because it has the characteristic of being purely quantitative and relational, having little to say of a qualitative, semantic nature and by that token being furthest from human subjectivity. Perhaps physics follows next because it deals only with the physical, inanimate world and, like chemistry, keeps its distance from us by its exclusive preoccupation with dead, inert matter. These sciences certainly seemed to have this connotation for Einstein who admitted that his commitment to science was a question of the flight from the 'I' and the 'We' to the 'It'.[23]

Perhaps much of what Trivers and Hamilton have been quoted as saying reduces to the realization that biology – particularly in its evolutionary aspects – comes much closer to subjective human concerns than do comparable sciences such as mathematics or physics.[24] Trivers himself seems to have emphasized this recently by echoing Freud's remarks about the progress of science quoted above and drawing an

[23] Quoted in S. J. Heims, *John Neumann and Norbert Wiener*, p. 116.

[24] Nevertheless, the example of Einstein's relativity and its temporary proscription in both Nazi Germany and the Soviet Union should remind us that even in modern times physics can encounter violent emotional resistance.

implicit equivalence between psychoanalysis and sociobio-logy.[25]

Yet in Comte's scientific hierarchy biology is not the ultimate science. This distinction is reserved for his own science, 'sociology', which will be to the modern world what theology was to the medieval – the Queen of the Sciences, the ultimate system of scientific truth, the positive study of the greatest, most complex and important reality known to man: society itself.

Such an idea appears to fit in well with Comte's belief in the inevitability of scientific progress from simple to com-plex sciences and from elemental ones to those which describe more elaborated phenomena such as organisms or societies. Yet it immediately brings us up against two para-doxes. The first is that his hierarchy assumes that sociology is founded on biology which, at least in its cultural-determinist or Marxist manifestations – in other words, all the important ones up to now – it most certainly is not, never has been and, if modern anti-biological prejudices hold their considerable sway, never will be. Secondly, Comte's and all subsequent sociologists' commitment to a cultural-determinist, group-orientated way of thinking clashes directly with the point which we have seen Trivers and Hamilton making about modern biology: that group- and species-advantage think-ing is fundamentally unscientific and designed to serve euphemistic, resisting and defensive tendencies which seek to make apologies for and to draw attention away from funda-mental scientific insights such as Darwinian evolution.

An example of what we are talking about can be found in Trivers' paper. He describes the case of infanticide by male langurs who, when they seize control of a harem from another male, set about killing all infants up to about the age of six months. In the past this had been used as an example of population-control in the interests of the group – an interpre-tation which clashes with Darwin's basic assumption of com-petition of each against all for individual reproductive

[25] R. Trivers, *Social Evolution*, pp. 46–7.

success. After demonstrating that the population-control-in-the-interests-of-the-group theory does not hold water, but that the basic Darwinian assumption does (because the male is liquidating the progeny of his predecessor in order all the quicker to establish his own), Trivers makes the following very telling point:

> in group- or species-advantage thinking, one individual's self-interest is typically elevated to that of the entire group. In this example, the adult male's self-interest has been elevated to that of the species. It is even given a new name; what he is concerned about is population regulation, something that is beneficial to all. The individual with the power to get away with murder becomes a benefactor, a patron of the weak and foolish. Elevating the self-interest of the powerful to that of the species tends to make the behaviour of the powerful appear justified. This must be one of the reasons for the popularity of species-advantage reasoning.[26]

The poverty of holism

If Comte had been right about his hierarchy of sciences, and if I am right in following Freud and attributing another factor – resistance – an important part in explaining the evolution of science, then here we have a major discrepancy. Putting aside the point made earlier about the presumed dependence of sociology on biology in the Comtean model, what are we to make of the assumption that, if sociology is the ultimate science, it should encounter ultimate resistance? For the simple truth of the matter is that it most decidedly does not. Admittedly, there is much resistance to and criticism of sociology within the scientific world and within Western societies as a whole, but then, so there is to other self-styled 'sciences' such as astrology and parapsychology. If we adhere to my argument that resistance to scientific insight increases

[26] Trivers, 'Sociobiology and Politics', pp. 6–7.

with convergence on human subjectivities and, at the same time, take Comte's hierarchy of sciences seriously, then we should expect sociology to suffer much worse from the sort of problems which Darwinian biology has encountered and should most definitely not expect it to manifest basic assumptions which contradict the biological foundations on which it should avowedly be built. Yet what we find in reality with regard to Comte's science of society is the exact opposite of this.

Far from being resisted because of its scientific insights, sociology is, by and large, welcomed because it makes dogmas of the very group- and species-advantage thinking which is so damaging to scientific progress in biology. From this point of view it seems that sociology as a so-called 'science' contains little or nothing in the way of genuine scientific insight but in reality functions as a vast defensive elaboration of the very type of cosy, euphemistic, tendentious ideas which Hamilton and Trivers so justly criticize in biology. It is a rationalized group–interest theory raised to the status of a dogmatic catechism, indeed, in some instances, to that of a secular religion.

To those unfamiliar with the history of sociology and unsympathetic to my line of reasoning it may come as a surprise to learn that Auguste Comte intended just this and made no secret of his religious pretentions when he styled himself 'Founder of the Positive Religion' and 'High Priest of Humanity'. Admittedly, by this time Comte was more than a little mad, but it would be a mistake to dismiss his prophetic pretentions as mere eccentricity. In many ways modern sociology shares many of the features of a religion, or at least, of its intellectually elaborated aspect – that is, *theology*. Indeed, this seems to be an inevitable consequence of the logic of Comte's argument. In the Middle Ages theology was the Queen of the Sciences because God, the subject of that science, was the ultimate reality. But in the nineteenth century Comte alleged what nearly all subsequent sociologists and what many others today still believe, namely, that society is the ultimate reality in human terms and that it is the origin of our values, science, our world-view, indeed, of our culture itself. In short, the dogma of cultural-determinism put 'culture' or 'society' or 'ideology' where God once had been and made these sociological entities play the determining, fateful role to which only real deities once aspired.

Emile Durkheim, the first sociologist to hold a university chair and the founder of what was to become, next to Marx's, the most influential paradigm of sociological explanation, openly proclaimed that there existed a collective consciousness which people worshipped in religion and which was – and, indeed, *ought* to be – the origin of all moral, aesthetic and cultural values. For Durkheim, the individual was born a clean slate to be written on by the collective consciousness, which, like God, was ultimately inexplicable because self-explicable, 'too complex' and 'beyond rational and critical explanation.'[27] This was cultural-determinism in one of its most extreme and influential forms.

It seems to have bothered this self-styled founder of scientific sociology remarkably little that such explanations as these take one very little further indeed if it is the very collective phenomena of society which call for explanation; for it is obvious that to explain one collective phenomenon – what Durkheim would have called the social fact – in terms of another one is to explain very little indeed. But here we have one of the most important characteristics of modern sociology and one which makes it very closely comparable to theology. This is what I would call its *holistic* aspect.

In this sense the term is usually opposed to reductionism: the doctrine that larger, more complex wholes can only be understood initially in terms of an analytic procedure in which they are broken down – reduced – to their simpler, constituent parts. In this sense reductionism is synonymous with scientific explanation. But in the sociological view, society is holistic: irreducible, unanalysable except in terms of other holistic concepts – in a phrase, 'more than the sum of its parts'.

[27] See C. Badcock, *Levi-Strauss*, pp. 26–8.

Looked at from another point of view, holism in the social sciences is always opposed to individualism: the idea that, since society is composed of individuals, it can only be understood in terms of those individuals. Succinctly summarizing the argument so far, we can say that Trivers and Hamilton were advocating individualism and reductionism in evolutionary biology, but that group-advantage thinking in biology and cultural-determinism in sociology represent holism and a prejudice against reductive explanation.

Survival of the inclusively fittest

In part, the holistic prejudices of modern sociology may be explained as a reaction against precisely the opposite tendency on the part of one of the other founding fathers of the discipline: Herbert Spencer. In stark contrast to Comte, Spencer insisted on an individualism which can only be called radical and which was to give what became known as *Social Darwinism* a distinctly bad name. It was not Darwin who coined the phrase 'Survival of the Fittest', but Spencer, who then went on to apply it – with notable imprecision about what it really meant – to human affairs, assuming that each individual's life was an evolutionary struggle against others and that the richest and most successful were therefore the 'winners' – the 'fittest' as confirmed by a social equivalent of natural selection.

In large part Spencer's crude Social Darwinism is the consequence of not realizing that 'fitness' as defined by evolutionary criteria is quite different from 'fitness' as equated with health, vigour and bodily well-being in general. According to Darwin, the fitness of an organism in the evolutionary sense can only be seen in relation to one factor: the number of descendants which it leaves – what is today often more accurately termed *reproductive success*.

The central principle of Darwinian evolution, natural selection, shows itself only in terms of differential survival: those organisms which leave more progeny than others are more 'fit' in the sense that they are better adapted to existing conditions than those which leave fewer. However, being fitted to survive in this sense, although suggesting enhanced health, vitality and general physical well-being, need not imply those things, at least as they are usually evaluated by human beings. For instance, on the strict Darwinian definition of 'fitness' – reproductive success – the fittest modern human beings are not to be found in the West as Spencer would have expected, but in the Third World where, despite shorter life-expectancy and considerably worse personal health, population expansion is much greater and reproductive success therefore more notable.

Again, it should not be assumed that our subjective perceptions of unfitness and ill-health are necessarily incompatible with the Darwinian meaning of 'fitness'. Consider the case of what is usually regarded as an instance of mild psychopathology in women who have just given birth: post-natal depression.

On the face of it this seems an obvious case of unfitness for the task of looking after the new-born baby, and many women clearly interpret it as such, much to their understandable distress. But there is another way of looking at it. It has recently been suggested that, far from being an instance of mild psychopathology, post-natal depression is in fact a classic Darwinian adaptation.[28] Here, evolutionary reasoning leads to a quite different view of the matter from common sense and proceeds as follows. In a species like our own, where maternal care is intensive, long-lasting and, in primal conditions, likely to induce a lengthy period of infertility caused by lactation, it will not necessarily promote a woman's Darwinian fitness as measured in terms of number of reproductively viable offspring to invest in raising young who are in any way unlikely to survive to adulthood. Therefore it might pay a mother to be somewhat dubious to begin

[28] M. de Vries, 'The Problem of Infanticide: A Reinterpretation of the Post-partum Attachment Period', in K. Immelman et al. (eds), *Behavioural Development: the Bielfeld Interdisciplinary Project*.

with in forming a strong attachment to her new-born child on the grounds that any deficiency or malformation in it might be evidence against its long-term viability and might increase the likelihood of rejection of the baby followed by a quick return to normal ovulation on the part of the mother. By contrast, a normal, healthy neonate with good survival prospects could presumably tolerate a day or two of relative neglect and begin to solicit more positive feelings in its mother once the initial phase of ambivalence was over.

In this instance what might be seen as promoting the mother's Darwinian fitness – post-natal depression – is most certainly not usually regarded as identical with health and well-being. On the contrary, much might be gained by not stigmatizing it as an illness, or still less evidence of a failing in those whom it affects, and instead regarding it as a more or less inevitable, hormonally-induced evolutionary adaptation whose value in the past was rather greater than it is today.

Another factor contributing both to the popularity of species-advantage holism and the notoriety of Social Darwinism brings us to the central theoretical concept of this book: the problem of *altruism*. Soldier ants which die protecting the nest, or sterile worker bees which spend their lives labouring for their fellows, exhibit altruism to a prodigious extent. Here, and throughout the subsequent argument, 'altruism' is defined as *an activity which promotes the fitness of the recipient at the expense of that of the provider*. 'Fitness' in Darwinian terms is measured, as we have just seen, purely by the number of surviving offspring which an organism has – in other words, in terms of its reproductive success. But how can Darwinian theory possibly hope to explain the evolution of such altruism if the practice of it actually *reduces* the fitness of the altruist? Evidently natural selection will discriminate against altruism as the following thought-experiment suggests.

Consider a population of organisms among whom no kind of altruism exists. Imagine that, perhaps by mutation, a gene for pure altruism appears in one or a small number of the members of the population. Since, by definition, such a gene will promote the fitness of the other, predominantly selfish genes in the population more than it will its own, altruism of this pure variety can hardly be expected to evolve. Exactly the same occurs if we picture the opposite situation: one in which we have a population entirely constituted by pure altruists. Here it will only take the chance appearance of a gene for selfishness to undermine the altruistic genes by an exactly comparable process – the latter will, by definition, promote the fitness of the gene for selfishness at their own expense and thereby ultimately bring about their own extinction. Unless we entertain discredited theories about group selectionism it follows as a matter of inexorable logic that pure altruism, uncontaminated by evolutionary self-interest, cannot possibly evolve and – if we ignore the human case for a moment – never seems to have done so.

In the light of considerations such as these it is not difficult to understand that altruism has been described as 'the central theoretical problem of sociobiology.'[29] Social Darwinists certainly failed to account for altruism in their enthusiasm for competition and the 'survival of the fittest' as they interpreted that phrase; but the holistic school also failed to take proper account of it, mainly because it seemed so obvious. By definition, altruism benefits others; the others are those who constitute the group or species. If selection operates at the level of the group or species it will select for altruism because that benefits the group. In short, if the community exists, altruism must evolve to serve it. Here altruism is no problem of any kind – it is an obvious adaptation.

But as far as genuine Darwinism is concerned altruism does constitute a real problem, as our thought-experiment illustrated. The beginning of a solution was suggested by W. D. Hamilton's concept of *inclusive fitness*. He showed that classical Darwinian fitness – reproductive success – could be favoured by altruistic sacrifice if that sacrifice promoted the reproductive success of genes which the altruist shared with

[29] E. O. Wilson, *Sociobiology*, p. 3.

the recipient of his altruism – an idea which has since become widely known as *kin altruism*, for obvious reasons.

An initial, instructive example of the principle of inclusive fitness and its application to kin altruism might be taken from the evolution of multicellular organisms. Herbert Spencer was convinced that the law of evolution determined that simplicity should be succeeded by complexity, and that unicellular organisms had to give way to multicellular ones, isolated multicellular organisms to social ones, simpler societies to more complex social forms and so on, so that the last could be seen as 'superorganisms' analogous, but intrinsically superior to their more primitive forerunners further down the evolutionary ladder. In taking this view he was guilty of a crude simplicity and lack of evolutionary advance in his own thinking which – ironically – was to make him commit an identical error to that of the holistic schools of sociological thought which took over his 'organismic analogy' of society as a complex, but integrated whole served by unproblematic altruism.

Yet, in genuinely Darwinian terms, we might wonder why cells in multicellular organisms should have evolved to cooperate and why some should have forgone the privilege of reproduction – and therefore their own reproductive success – for the benefit of others. As we have already noticed, it would seem that if natural selection requires reproductive success such altruism could not evolve.

However that may be, 'the key fact regarding cells in our body is that *all are identically related.*'

Thus, in the early evolution of multicellular organisms, a cell was selected to forgo reproduction whenever it transferred a benefit to the reproducing cells greater than the cost (to its own reproductive success) suffered. All efficient interactions were favoured, and there rapidly developed a set of somatic cells that did not reproduce, but that helped sustain the germinal cells that did reproduce. Since the interests of all cells are identical (because of their genetic identity), specialization evolves without conflict. The kidney and the liver are not in

conflict with each other over how many nutrients to remove
from the bloodstream; both have been selected to remove the
amount of nutrients that maximizes the reproductive interests
of the larger unit.[30]

In short, an organism, be it a single cell within a larger
organism or a multicellular organism itself, might evolve
altruism if by doing so it promoted the reproductive success
of its own genes for altruism present in its relatives to a
greater extent than if it were to reproduce itself. Since the
successfully-reproducing organism is presumed to share
genes identical to those of the altruist which had to forgo
reproduction, selection would not discriminate against them:
on the contrary, under these conditions the altruist's service
on behalf of its genes present in its relative would actually
promote its reproductive success more than if it were to
reproduce itself. In a phrase, such altruism would promote
the organism's *inclusive fitness*: that measure of its reproductive success which it shared with related organisms; as a form
of altruism it would be altruism directed towards *kin*.[31]

Another example, and one, furthermore, featuring a
society in the more usual sense of the word, might be provided by the case which I mentioned when first introducing
the whole issue of altruism: the social insects. If ever there
was an example which appeared to merit the holistic, group-
advantage or superorganic approach it is surely this. Here in
reality are societies which, in their elaborate integration, high
degree of differentiation and division of labour, altruism and

[30] Trivers, *Social Evolution*, p. 135, italics and parentheses mine.

[31] However, it is important to notice that mere genetic kinship is not
enough to cause organisms to promote their inclusive fitness through
altruistic behaviour, as is obvious if one considers the possibility that the
genes shared in common code for *selfishness*. Similarly, the presence of a
gene for altruism could promote the inclusive fitness of members of a
population under certain conditions even if they were not close kin.
Nevertheless, the latter does not mean that pure altruism is sustainable
since the thought- experiment described above can be run assuming genes
for kin altruism in place of those for selfishness, with the same results. See
R. Dawkins, 'Twelve Misunderstandings of Kin Selection', *Zeitschrift fur
Tierpsychologie*, 51, 1979, pp. 184–200.

cooperation, represent the ideal social systems imagined by sociologists of the holistic, cultural-determinist school. Here the frequently-voiced criticisms which apply when these social systems are posited for human societies cut no ice at all: there is no problem of social conflict, crime or deviance; no social change; no technological innovation; no complications of a psychological or philosophical nature; no religious dimension; no drag of tradition and no problem of politics. Here we find a society which genuinely resembles a single, functioning organism; where every part is dependent on every other and in which the stability, unity and integration of the system is about as fully developed as it could be. Here as nowhere else we encounter selfless commitment by the members to the good of the social whole: suicidal self-sacrifice by soldiers, tireless labour by workers, unremitting reproduction of the population by the queen, a general harmony and systematic interaction of all the parts to form a social whole of truly impressive coherence and stability. Here, if nowhere else, Spencer's concept of the superorganic social whole seems to be justified, and it is here that we would have expected the idea to have had its greatest success.

Nevertheless, if, in taking account of *inclusive* fitness as explained above, we expand the concept of fitness to cover not merely individuals' own genes, but also those which they share in common with relatives, then it follows that because of a peculiarity of reproduction among the Hymenoptera, worker bees or ants are more closely related to their sisters than to any offspring which they might engender themselves (sisters share on average three-quarters of their genes, but a worker's offspring would only inherit one-half of them). More of the hymenopteran worker's genes will be represented in the next generation if, rather than raise her own young, she instead raises those of her own mother (the queen). In this way selection might favour the evolution of sterile castes of daughters of a single, reproductive mother – something which appears to have occurred a number of times among hymenopteran species, although rarely elsewhere.

Looked at from this perspective, the evolutionary mechanism involved is most emphatically not a holistic one, nor is it a narrowly individualistic one which assumes that the 'survival of the fittest' cannot explain social cooperation except by speaking in terms of the 'superorganism'. On the contrary, it is the classical Darwinian one: reproductive success – fitness in the evolutionary sense – except expanded to become inclusive fitness and to take into account the reproductive success not merely of an organism's own genes, but those which it shares with relatives. Essentially it is a type of explanation which comes to see the organism as existing ultimately for the benefit of its genes rather than vice versa.

The bee-hive has often been seen as a model for the ideal human society, with the queen ruling imperiously for the good of the community and the workers cooperating without dissent. From one point of view it looks like an idealized monarchy or archetypal fascist state: the ruler rules, all others obey; yet, from another point of view one could see it as a workers' tyranny, with the sterile castes farming the queen for progeny out of pure evolutionary self-interest. In reality, it now looks as if both views are partly true and partly false: because of some measure of genetic disparity between queen, workers and drones, conflict and exploitation certainly can exist. Truer is the view that both ruler and ruled, queen and workers are being exploited, not so much by one another, but by the genes which they hold in common and which cause them to specialize in the roles assigned to them by the peculiarities of hymenopteran reproduction. If there is any element of sacrifice for a more profound reality it is sacrifice of the individual organism for the benefit of the replication and survival of its genes, rather than for the replication or survival of the group or the species.

If the individual organism or some group of organisms was the principal unit on which selective forces came to bear, inclusive fitness would not be as powerful an explanatory concept as it is. For if, as Spencer implicitly supposed, evolution only took account of individual organisms, irrespective of their genetic interrelations, relatives with whom an organism shared some of its genes would be no different from completely unrelated organisms, and hence certain phenomena – like altruism, for instance – would be hard to explain. (As we have just seen, Spencer could only explain it by reproducing the idea of the individual organism at a higher level: the superorganic, social one.) Yet if the group were the evolutionary unit the relatedness of individuals within it would not matter, and once again the concept of inclusive fitness would carry no weight. The fact that it has largely revolutionized our understanding of the evolution of fundamental adaptive traits for social living such as altruism argues strongly for it and against the idea that it is the individual or the group on which evolution ultimately operates.

Evolution and the significance of life

The concept of inclusive fitness, Mendel's laws of inheritance and our modern understanding of the nature of the genetic code all work together to press the conclusion that organisms have evolved to be little more than the elaborate packaging and guardians of their genes. To put the matter succinctly, one might answer the old conundrum about which came first, the chicken or the egg, by saying that from the perspective of modern evolutionary biology the chicken is the egg's way of making another egg.[32]

Consider one of the most simple and fully understood of self-replicating organisms: the T4 bacteriophage. This is a virus which attacks the common human gut-bacterium, *Escherichia coli*. It consists of a length of DNA, the organic polymer which carries genetic information encoded in the sequence of bases joined to its sugar-phosphate helical strands. The DNA of the virus is contained within a polygonal protein container which is joined via a short collar to a

---

[32] Wilson, *Sociobiology*, p. 3.

tube which ends in an array of spikes by means of which the bacteriophage attaches itself to the bacterium's surface. If the virus successfully infects the bacterium the tube connected to the head penetrates the cell wall of the host and injects the naked DNA into the bacterial cytoplasm. Here it uses the cell machinery of the bacterium to make copies of itself: DNA, polygonal head, tube, collar, and so on. The parts become assembled into new bacteriophages and eventually, when perhaps two hundred or more have been made, the bacterial cell wall breaks and the new viral particles spill out to begin the cycle once again.

Now admittedly, the T4 bacteriophage is different in some ways from higher organisms such as plants, animals or humans. Because it cannot move itself and go in search of nutrients it has no need of the elaborate means of motility, sensory perception and behaviour which an animal must have if it is to eat. Because it is not a plant it cannot build up nutrients in its own tissues and therefore needs none of the elaborate cellular machinery and structural forms found in plants. Because it takes in no nutrients whatsoever it cannot repair itself, grow independently or change in any way once it has been constituted. Therefore it needs none of the complex repair, maintenance and control mechanisms which operate in the higher organisms which have these abilities. Because it does not reproduce sexually the T4 bacteriophage has no need to search for a mate, and because it reproduces within another organism, using that organism's life-processes for its own ends, it need not lay eggs, gestate young or even undergo fission into two exact copies of itself.

Yet for all this, and as far as evolution is concerned, the T4 bacteriophage is the same as any other organism, and evolutionary principles which apply to much more complex organisms also apply to it. This is because it fulfils, albeit it in a very simple and parasitical way, the basic function of any organism: it provides a more-or-less elaborate protein packaging for the genetic information which it contains within it and provides a means of ensuring the replication of that genetic information in the future. The fact that it lacks all the peripheral paraphernalia that make it so apparently unlike a higher organism such as a human being is, from the biological point of view, really much less important than it seems. From the all-important point of view of evolution, the T4 bacteriophage and a human being are functionally identical: both are protein-packaged, organismic encapsulations of the vital element in evolution: genetic information. The fact that human beings are such complex encapsulating organisms and the T4 bacteriophage such a simple one is neither here nor there as far as evolution is concerned. Both are the expression of genetic information which has survived; both survive because they express genetic information. This is the essence of the Darwinian view of evolution.

It now seems that modern evolutionary biology can answer not merely the chicken-and-egg conundrum but that it can also give some sort of objective and factually well-founded answer to the ultimate question: 'Why are we here?' (something to be especially welcomed, many would say, given the sort of fantastic nonsense which has been used to answer this question in the past). Today we can answer this question with brutal frankness: we are here to reproduce ourselves; we are providing a temporary home for our genes; life is ultimately only a very complex process of transmission of genetic information to future generations which is itself only a complex biochemical concomitant of the resurfacing of our planet brought about ultimately by nuclear fusion in the sun and nuclear fission in the interior of the earth.

Of course, these answers, although demonstrably correct from the point of view of modern science, are not complete. We might go on to ask why the sun shines; indeed, why it, or indeed anything else, exists in the first place?

To these ultimate questions we may never know the answers, indeed, such answers may not ultimately exist. But this need not trivialize or invalidate the answers given by modern science about evolution, the significance of life, its dependence on the sun, and so on. These remain valid answers, at least until they are proved to be wrong, inadequate or incomplete. For the time being, evolutionary theory, Mendelian genetics and modern biochemistry seem to produce one conclusion of which we can be reasonably confident: that evolution acts ultimately on units of genetic information and that organisms can only be understood as temporary carriers of that information. This successfully explains both their origin, their evolution and their function. There is simply no other credible answer.

Of course, this answer to the question of life is not particularly gratifying, especially when compared with some of the grandiose, romantic answers which have been given in the past. For instance, if I am nothing other than packaging for my genes, does that make me, from the point of view of the history of life at least, just like any piece of packaging which for a while serves its purpose but is then thoughtlessly discarded once its purpose is fulfilled? This reminder of my inevitable mortality and inconsequence is bound to be disconcerting.

Again, the idea is insulting to my opinion of myself. Evolutionary theory may tell me that I am only a very much more complex version of something essentially like a T4 bacteriophage, but this is hardly gratifying to my subjective evaluation of my importance. Here, whichever way I approach it, I encounter that blow to my naïve self-love of which we saw Freud speak when he tried to account for the resistance to the discoveries of Copernicus and Darwin, not to mention to those of himself. All the more understandable is it then that many people, when confronted with such ungratifying answers to the deep questions of life, prefer to console themselves with comforting ideas of some special creation by a reassuringly anthropomorphic God, or even that some biologists should, as we have seen, prefer the idea of group- or species-selection. In its avoidance of reductionism to the level of the individual and the gene the latter also serves to fend off the disquieting consciousness of the dependence of higher biological functions on lower, more basic ones. Furthermore, it serves to place a fig-leaf over the most unmentionable element of all – the essential selfishness which underlies what passes for altruism. With altruism serving the interests of the group and evolution acting like a benign father-figure in 'improving' the species one could almost believe that the old myths were true after all and that God, or at least something recognizably like him, was still in his heaven and that all that was altruistic was right with the world.

Darwinian fitness and Freudian libido

If we reflect for a moment on the human, psychological consequences of the modern Darwinian view of evolution we will perhaps begin to see that Freud is linked to Darwin by much more than the common theme of resistance to scientific insight which offends human vanity. If human beings, like all other organisms and like the T4 viral particle, evolved to pass on their genes to their successors then one would expect that evolution must have imposed two principal requirements on them from the behavioural point of view. These two requirements are that they should discharge their obligations to their genes both by safeguarding them – which in practice means safeguarding themselves and their relatives – and by reproducing themselves. If this were true then we should expect to find two fundamental behavioural propensities deeply engrained in the nature of all higher organisms which had the ability both to protect, feed and repair themselves and which experienced the necessity of sexual reproduction. We should expect them to possess genetically-programmed instincts for self-preservation and for reproductive activities. It is therefore not surprising that Freud, as a result of his psychological investigations into human beings, came to think that men and women were motivated by two principal types of instincts: so-called ego-instincts directed to self-preservation, and sexual or libidinal ones directed ultimately to reproduction.[33]

[33] Here I ignore the life/death instinct dichotomy which Freud developed later in his life and which I do not believe has any foundation in biological reality. For a further discussion see p. 160 below.

Since in the case of human beings the self-preservative instincts ultimately come to serve the reproductive ones (because it is the genes, after all, and not the individual organism, which is handed on), the prominence of the libido in the Freudian view of human nature is inevitable and natural. It simply reflects the paramount necessity of organic existence as we have been discussing it here – the fact that the individual organism is only a temporary packaging for its genes:

> The individual himself regards sexuality as one of his own ends; whereas from another point of view he is an appendage to his germ-plasm, at whose disposal he puts his energies in return for a bonus of pleasure. He is the mortal vehicle of a (possibly) immortal substance – like the inheritor of an entailed property, who is only the temporary holder of an estate which survives him.[34]

When it was first put forward by Freud the libido theory was hotly denied and, rather like Darwin's idea (of which it was, in the sense being discussed here, an inevitable consequence), has never been fully accepted by more than a few. Earlier in this century resistance to it chiefly centred on its findings regarding the sexual life of children and the fact that the sexual drive is more widely associated with aspects of the body and mind than merely those which narrowly serve the obvious reproductive function. Today infantile sexuality is seldom denied, probably because it is such an undeniable fact, particularly in the current permissive climate of child-rearing; and fashionable sexual-deviations of various kinds have made the concept of a wider scope to human sexuality less of an affront.

But the libido theory remains, like Darwin's evolutionary theory to which we now see it is so closely akin, very much an unwelcome blow to human vanity and moral pretentiousness. It is something which men – and perhaps especially a

[34] S. Freud, 'On Narcissism', XIV, 78.

vociferous minority of modern *women* – still find unacceptable. Writing about the libido theory recently Anna Freud commented that

> Disbelief and indignation now come from a new side and are directed to different aims: the side of the modern women's liberation movement which disputes Freud's theory of female sexuality and its development. Representatives of this movement experience this theory as an affront and depreciation, very similar to how formerly the representatives of the idea of 'innocent childhood' reacted to the theory of infantile sexuality . . . They deny the existence of any inherited difference between men and women and explain the appearance of early unlikeness as the exclusive result of social influences on upbringing which push the girl to play with dolls and propel the boy toward an interest in motors, soldiers, and war games. The anatomical difference between penis and vagina, between impregnation and giving birth, and its decisive impact on psychic development are pushed aside in the passionate efforts to free women from the subjugation in which they have in fact been held for centuries and to put women in a position that in every respect equals that of their male partners.[35]

Once again we find the now familiar picture: holistic cultural-determinism is used to discount the individualism and reductionism of the modern biological and psychoanalytic accounts of sexuality. Here again, modern evolutionary biology and psychoanalysis are closely in agreement, and it is no accident that biologists frequently incur the wrath of the sexual progressives almost as much as the Freudians do. Indeed, recently one of them has actually had the courage to affirm this agreement in print. Following a line of argument exactly like mine and pointing out that

> much of being human consists of contributing to the success of our genes just as being a kangaroo, or even a dandelion

[35] A. Freud, 'A Study-guide to Freud's Writings', in *Psychoanalytic Psychology of Normal Development*, pp. 235–6.

involves contributing to the success of kangaroo and dande-
lion genes

David Barash candidly concludes, 'Freud was right: much of
our behaviour has to do with sex.'[36]

It seems that some members of the women's movement
are so profoundly convinced that differences between the
sexes imply female inferiority that they feel the need to deny
that any differences exist at all – at least, in principle. Where
they undeniably do exist in practice, cultural-determinism
comes triumphantly to the rescue: sex-differences are purely
cultural – in other words, they are arbitrary conventions
which can be changed at will! Furthermore, this prejudice is
obstinately retained, despite overwhelming factual evidence
to the contrary.

Apologists for cultural-determinism frequently take refuge
in the belief that, since culture and its determining influence
are so pervasive, no real test of the validity of any other view
is possible. For instance, on the question of sexual orien-
tation, they would probably argue that the only way to
resolve the issue definitely would be to carry out a thor-
oughly impossible experiment in which a number of chromosomal males were born appearing like females and a
corresponding group of chromosomal females were born
resembling males. If each group were unambiguously social-
ized up to adolescence in accordance with their apparent sex
the relative weighting of cultural and natural determinants of
sexual behaviour could be evaluated.

Another frequently-heard prejudice is that it is absurd to
imagine that single genes can influence behaviour, and that
therefore genetic determinism of anything beyond trivial
traits such as eye-colour can be discounted altogether.
Although I would not want to encourage the equally-mis-
guided prejudices of crude biological determinism (for
instance, on the important issue of incest-avoidance), it must
nevertheless be pointed out that here, as elsewhere, cultural-
determinism has got it wrong. The apparently impossible

[36] D. Barash, *Sociobiology: The Whisperings Within*, p. 40.

experiment suggested above has been carried out (at least, as far as the male half of it is concerned) by virtue of the determining effects of a single recessive gene (that coding for the enzyme, 5α-reductase).

A study conducted in the Dominican Republic recently identified eighteen male pseudo-hermaphrodites who, because of this congenital enzyme deficiency, were born looking like females and were raised accordingly. By contrast to some previously reported cases, normal hormonal activity was allowed to occur at puberty because no one suspected that the subjects were anything other than female. The study showed that sixteen out of eighteen subjects unambiguously raised as girls (i.e., 89 per cent of the sample) changed to a male gender-role at puberty, despite parental consternation and considerable social pressure to the contrary. 'The ages at which subjects first experienced morning erections, nocturnal emissions, masturbation and sexual intercourse were not appreciably different between those raised as girls who changed to a male-gender identity' and a control group raised as boys.[37] The study concluded that it was the extent of exposure to hormonal rather than cultural influences which finally determined sexual identity and behaviour in the sample.

By contrast to these very significant scientific findings, cultural-determinism perseveres in the belief that culture rather than biology determines gender identity. The individual is seen as the passive victim of cultural determinants so that social pressure and parental conditioning – the very factors shown to yield to hormonal contradiction in the majority of cases in the Dominican Republic study – are what determine whether one behaves as a male or a female.

In complete contrast to this view, both modern evolutionary biology and Freudian psychoanalysis are in agreement about one thing: that sexual differences are to a large extent

[37] J. Imperato-McGinley et al., 'Androgens and the Evolution of Male-gender Identity among Male Pseudohermaphrodites with a 5α-reductase Deficiency', *The New England Journal of Medicine*, Vol. 300, no. 22, 1979, p. 1234.

innate and tend to form cultural conventions as much, if not more, than they are formed by them. As far as modern biology is concerned, Trivers' influential theory of parental investment suggests that, because each sex has a different investment of time, energy, exposure to danger and so on in its sex cells and eventual offspring, then each sex will behave differently compared to the other and that, as Trivers puts it, 'even when ostensibly cooperating in a joint task male and female interests are rarely identical.'[38]

This explains why females in so many species are notably 'coy' (by which I mean they show a relative choosiness about mating) when compared with males. Since the female tends to have relatively few sex cells, which are released relatively rarely compared to those of males and – especially in mammalian species – may have to undertake long internal gestation of the young followed by a heavy commitment to feeding, it follows that it will pay her to be relatively discerning regarding the choice of a mate since an unfit or otherwise inferior male threatens her own very considerable investment in the young. The male, on the other hand, with his numerous and 'cheap' sex cells may, particularly if he contributes little to raising the young, be generally indiscriminate about his mates. In this circumstance, he may also find himself in conflict with other males who are bent on similar campaigns of indiscriminate mass-fertilization. This will have important consequences for sexual selection and for male and female sexual behaviour, anatomy and the development of sexual dimorphism and secondary sexual characteristics in general. It will most certainly not produce identity of sexual behaviour, anatomy or psychology, and if this is true of other animals there is no reason why it should not be true of human beings.

In a similar way, psychoanalytic investigations find that males and females are constituted in part at least in different

---

[38] R. Trivers, 'Parental Investment and Sexual Selection' in B. Campbell (ed.), *Sexual Selection and the Descent of Man*, p. 174.

ways and that a fundamental biological substrate of 'masculinity' and 'feminity' seems to exist. Nevertheless, important differences do remain between some aspects of Freudian and modern biological theory, particularly on the issue of the extent and the nature of biological, genetic 'programming' of human beings. But before we come to consider these controversies, let us first turn our attention to another respect in which modern evolutionary biology has come closely to resemble Freudian psychoanalysis and has, indeed, converged on its central finding: the existence of the dynamic unconscious. For it should not surprise us to find that if, as we saw earlier, some modern sociobiologists have had recourse to the idea of *resistance* – that most despised and allegedly 'unscientific' of psychoanalytic concepts – then one or two of them might begin to ponder the value of that equally controversial psychoanalytic conception of which resistance is only one highly specialized example – I refer, of course, to the fundamental Freudian concept of *repression*.

The General Theory of Altruism

1

Reciprocal Altruism, Repression and Regression

The rediscovery of the unconscious

In the previous chapter we saw how the concept of kin altruism explains one important form of self-sacrifice: altruism in the interests of genes which are shared in common with relatives. We also saw how the extended notion of fitness – inclusive fitness – could accommodate such altruistic behaviours within an authentic Darwinian perspective.

Yet not all acts of altruism seen in animal populations – not to mention among human beings – can be accounted for on this basis. Sometimes altruistic interactions occur between organisms which are not related particularly closely, or which may be totally unrelated. Dolphins and whales, for instance, are notable for coming to the aid of others who may on occasions belong to different species – a behaviour which may well underlie stories of their rescue of humans. Again, on coral reefs fish such as groupers are subject to the attention of cleaner wrasses which literally clean up the mouth and gill cavities of the larger fish. This, like the previous example, is an instance, not of kin altruism, but of *reciprocal altruism*.

In cases of reciprocal altruism one organism performs a service or makes a sacrifice for another organism which then reciprocates in some way so that the sacrifice of the provider is balanced by a corresponding service or sacrifice by the recipient. In the case of the grouper and cleaner wrasse, the grouper is relieved of parasites and remains of decaying food etc., while the cleaner gets a meal. In such relationships evidently both parties stand to gain and so here, once again, there is no problem as far as the Darwinian paradigm is concerned: reciprocal altruism might evolve to meet the needs of the organisms concerned in such a way that any sacrifice by one party is compensated for by a provision of the other.

Robert Trivers, to whom we owe our most important insights into reciprocal altruism,[1] did not fail to notice that this is a form of altruism most particularly relevant to human societies and widely practised within them. He lists the following examples: helping in times of danger or distress; sharing food; sharing implements; sharing knowledge.[2] However, he expresses the opinion that 'The strongest argument for the operation of reciprocal altruistic selection in humans is the psychological system controlling some forms of human altruism.'[3]

This comes about because it is clear that reciprocal altruism, perhaps more than any other kind of interaction between organisms, creates many possibilities for error, mistakes, inadequate or nil reciprocation, and, above all, *cheating*. If one party to a reciprocal interaction can get away with the benefit to itself without paying the cost to the other then, obviously, its fitness is likely to be promoted and that of its cheated partner reduced. To return to the grouper/cleaner-wrasse example for a moment, it is interesting to note that groupers are occasionally preyed upon by another small fish (the so-called 'false cleaner', *Aspidontus taeniatus*) which resembles the authentic cleaner in shape and coloration but, once it has secured access to its host, takes a bite out of it and vanishes, leaving the grouper nursing a wound and deprived of a service. Trivers distinguishes between what he calls 'gross' and 'subtle' cheating and points out that in the latter

[1] R. Trivers, 'The Evolution of Reciprocal Altruism', *Quarterly Review of Biology*, 46, 1971, pp. 35–57; and *Social Evolution*, pp. 47–9, 361–94.

[2] R. Trivers, 'Sociobiology and Politics', in E. White (ed.), *Sociobiology and Human Politics*, p. 10.

[3] Ibid., p. 11.

case where, unlike the former, the cheater does reciprocate something, albeit less than he should,

> It is the subtlety of the discrimination necessary to detect this form of cheating and the awkward situation that ensues that permit some subtle cheating to be adaptive. This sets up a dynamic tension in the system that has important repercussions.[4]

Some of the most important of these repercussions affect the psychological system underlying human reciprocal altruism:

> Given this unstable character of the system, where a degree of cheating is adaptive, natural selection will rapidly favour a complex psychological system in each individual regulating both his own altruistic and cheating tendencies and his responses to these tendencies in others. As selection favours subtler forms of cheating, it will favour more acute abilities to detect cheating. The system that results should simultaneously allow the individual to reap the benefits of altruistic exchanges, to protect himself from gross and subtle forms of cheating, and to practise those forms of cheating that local conditions make adaptive. Individuals will differ not in being altruists or cheaters, but in the degree of altruism they show and in the conditions under which they will cheat.[5]

He goes on to point out that the system might select for friendliness towards altruists, but what he calls 'moralistic aggression' against cheats. In the case of the aggrieved grouper mentioned earlier we might well imagine that had he been equipped with human psychological proclivities the experience of being cheated and wounded by the false cleaner might have left him with a strong sense of angry resentment. It follows that resentful anger at being tricked is highly

[4] Ibid., p. 13.
[5] Ibid., p. 15.

adaptive for organisms with complex psychologies, frequent and complex reciprocal interactions and a need to protect themselves from both gross and subtle cheating. Similarly, gratitude and sympathy may be adaptive in other circumstances where the display of these reactions will secure present or future advantages for the subject in complex reciprocal relationships. Even anger directed at oneself in the form of guilt and remorseful feelings becomes understandable on this basis: these responses function to control reactions of one's own to situations where, for instance, one becomes aware that others have caught one cheating or failing to reciprocate adequately and the situation demands some act of reparation or expiation in one's own interests, quite apart from that of the aggrieved parties.

Nevertheless, the 'dynamic tension of the system' to which we saw Trivers referring earlier will not let it rest there because

> Once friendship, moralistic aggression, guilt, sympathy, and gratitude have evolved to regulate the altruistic system, selection will favour mimicking these traits in order to influence the behaviour of others to one's own advantage. Apparent acts of generosity and friendship may induce genuine friendship and altruism in return. Sham moralistic aggression when no real cheating has occurred may nevertheless induce reparative altruism. Sham guilt may convince a wronged friend that one has reformed one's ways even when the cheating is about to be resumed. Likewise, selection will favour the hypocrisy of pretending one is in dire circumstances in order to induce sympathy-motivated altruistic behaviour. Finally, mimicking sympathy may give the appearance of helping in order to induce reciprocity; and mimicking gratitude may mislead an individual into expecting he will be reciprocated.[6]

The consequence of all this is that, from the psychological point of view, human beings need to adopt a very subtle, sophisticated approach to reciprocal interactions which, given their endemic nature in human life, means that such psychological adaptations must have become of paramount

[6] Ibid., p. 19.

importance. Quite apart from the need to detect cheating and to display the range of emotional responses which the system of reciprocal altruism may demand, human beings would also need to be equipped with such attributes as excellent memory (because reciprocation often follows much later), an ability to calculate costs and rewards (because many inter-actions will be with more than one party, perhaps on more than one occasion and through more than one medium), and, above all, what Trivers calls 'developmental plasticity of those traits regulating both altruistic and cheating tendencies and responses to these tendencies in others'.[7] He concludes his original paper with the remark that

> Given the psychological and cognitive complexity the system rapidly requires, one may wonder to what extent the impor-tance of altruism in human evolution set up a selection pres-sure for psychological and cognitive powers that partly contributed to the large increase in hominid brain size during the Pleistocene.[8]

Yet, quite apart from these largely cognitive consider-ations, it is possible that the modern sociobiological view of altruism may entail a more dynamic approach to psychology:

> I suggest that the separateness of our individual self-interests, and the conflicts among us that derive from this separateness, have created a social milieu in which, paradoxically, the only way we can actually maximize our own self-interest and deceive successfully is by continually denying – at least in certain arenas – that we are doing such things. By conveying the impression that we do not intend to deceive, and that we are in fact altruistic and have the interests of others at heart, we actually advance our own (evolutionary) self-interest. I believe as a consequence that our general cleverness at cre-ating deceptions and detecting them has made it next to impossible for individuals to benefit from deliberate decep-tion in ordinary social situations, because of the likelihood of detection and exposure, and, possibly, severe punishment.

[7] Ibid., p. 23.
[8] Ibid., p. 25.

The result, I believe, is that in our social scenario-building we have evolved to deceive even ourselves about our true motives.[9]

In the course of additional reflections on the question of reciprocal altruism added to a reprinting of parts of his original paper on the subject (and, evidently, as a continuation of the line of thought just quoted), Trivers adds the following, very significant observation:

Of particular importance to cheating is the self-deception that it automatically tends to generate. Since it is useful to maintain a facade of morality and public beneficence, cheating must be disguised – increasingly, even to the actor himself. The actor becomes less and less conscious of the true nature of his actions.[10]

Later he adds that

As mechanisms for spotting deception become more subtle, organisms may be selected to render some facts and motives unconscious, the better to conceal deception. In the broadest sense, the organism is selected to become unconscious of some of its deception, in order not to betray, by signs of self-knowledge, the deceptions being practised.

With the advent of language in the human lineage, the possibilities for deception and self-deception were greatly enlarged.[11]

Nobody would doubt that it was the discovery of the unconscious which was Freud's greatest and central achievement. However, in saying this one must stress that the unconscious which Freud discovered was in certain crucial respects different from what we might call the merely 'descriptive' unconscious which had long been known to art, literature and philosophy, if not in any important sense to science. This 'descriptive' unconscious is exactly what its name implies: a purely nominal mental category covering all

[9] R. D. Alexander, *Darwinism and Human Affairs*, p. 134.

[10] Trivers, 'Sociobiology and Politics', p. 26.

[11] Ibid., p. 35.

that can be described as not included in consciousness. If this is all that Trivers intended, then his mention of it would not in any way necessarily call Freud and psychoanalysis to mind. But Trivers' use of the term 'unconscious' is much more than purely descriptive and shows all the characteristics of its use in psychoanalysis and reflects what is most distinctive of Freud's concept: that the unconscious is *dynamic*, and *topographical*.

The essentially dynamic nature of Trivers' unconscious is fully apparent in the previous quotations where, as we have seen, he describes the unconscious, not merely as something apart from consciousness, but as a phenomenon positively engendered by the need to hide certain realities from consciousness – in a word, as a consequence of *repression*.

This is exactly like Freud's use of the term 'unconscious', especially in the first period of psychoanalysis, where the unconscious was principally regarded as the recipient of repressed material and its associated instinctual trends: '*the essence of repression lies simply in turning something away, and keeping it at a distance from consciousness.*'[12] At the end of his life when, as we shall see later, the concept of repression had become elaborated in terms of the more general idea of mechanisms of defence, Freud made a point exactly like that of Trivers when he observed that 'the defensive mechanisms of the ego are condemned to falsify one's internal perception and to give one only an imperfect and distorted picture of one's id.'[13]

Even the notion that such repressions of the conscious into the unconscious may be pathological and maladaptive in nature, so central to Freud's early view of psychopathology, finds an echo in Trivers' article when he says that

self-deception induces a range of impaired learning that may have costs far removed from the initial acts generating the impulse toward self-deception.[14]

[12] S. Freud, 'Repression', XIV, 147 (Freud's italics).
[13] S. Freud, 'Analysis Terminable and Interminable', XXIII, 237.
[14] Trivers, 'Sociobiology and Politics', p. 26

Or, as Freud put it:

> The mechanisms of defence . . . may become dangers in themselves. It sometimes turns out that the ego has paid too high a price for the services they render it. The dynamic expenditure necessary for maintaining them, and the restrictions of the ego which they almost invariably entail, prove a heavy burden on the psychical economy.[15]

Trivers' view of the unconscious is also *topographical* – that is, related to different levels or regions of consciousness and unconsciousness:

> A portion of the brain devoted to verbal functions must become specialized for the manufacture and maintenance of falsehoods. This will require biased perceptions, biased memory, and biased logic; and these processes are ideally kept unconscious.[16]

Freud certainly agreed that internal differentiations of consciousness and function were necessary for the dynamic unconscious to be able to operate, and he also agreed that this would inevitably involve differential and tendentious registration of perceptions, memories and so on, even though he would have been more cautious about trying to localize such functions in the brain.

Finally, in commenting that

> The mind must be structured in a very complex fashion, repeatedly split into public and private portions, with complicated interactions between the subsections[17]

Trivers is suggesting a psychological model which, as he notes elsewhere,[18] is closely comparable to that which Freud conceived when he produced his famous structural description of a mind split, not merely between conscious, pre-

---

[15] S. Freud, 'Analysis', XXIII, 237.
[16] Trivers, 'Sociobiology and Politics', p. 35
[17] Ibid., p. 35.
[18] Trivers, *Social Evolution*, p. 163. See below p. 65.

conscious and unconscious, but between psychic agencies such as the id, ego and superego. In a similar way Barash also observes that

> our consciousness could be similar to the Freudian superego, selected to ride herd on the subconscious, a ravening core of socially disruptive fitness maximizing, which must exist if we are to achieve evolutionary success but which must also be kept below the surface for the same reason. (This argument has the interesting consequence that human beings may differ from other animals not in the elaboration of consciousness, but rather, in the extent of their unconscious, since in general, animals have less need of deceit.)[19]

I entitled this section 'The rediscovery of the unconscious' because it seems to me that, in a way which is not without precedents in the history of science, modern biology can be credited with something of an original and largely underivative rediscovery of what is perhaps the most important single fact about human psychology: that the greater and most significant part of it functions unconsciously and dynamically. Indeed, it may well be that eventually this rediscovery of the fundamental premise of psychoanalysis by modern biology will be seen to have signalled the beginning of the end of the period of latency of psychoanalysis as an accepted science, much as both Copernican astronomy and Darwinian evolution were to be accepted after periods of latency of comparable duration.

To those who might be tempted to object that no one can in any really meaningful way rediscover what has been discovered already, let me quote what I regard as a persuasive analogy. At the beginning of this century Albert Einstein published an epoch-making paper on the 'photo-electric effect' which, in principle, was a rediscovery of the corpuscular theory of light first put forward in a rigorous scientific way by Isaac Newton some two hundred years earlier. In the intervening centuries, the wave-theory of light had become

[19] D. Barash, *Sociobiology and Behaviour*, p. 157.

dominant and Newton's particle-theory ignored and forgotten. With Einstein's paper, the particle-theory of light came back and the quantum of electro-magnetic radiation became habitually known as the *photon* which, following the researches of Einstein and others, was now known to exhibit particulate properties, quite apart from its other wave-like features.

I call this a 'rediscovery' of the particle-theory of light because it had three essential characteristics: first, the theory formed part of a completely new paradigm in physics, one quite distinct from and in certain respects even opposed to, that of Newton; secondly, Einstein discovered it investigating effects unknown to Newton with techniques not in existence in the latter's time; and thirdly, the original idea had been so apparently decisively disproved and discounted that any resurrection of it had all the hall-marks of an original and indeed revolutionary scientific discovery.

So, perhaps, it is with the modern biological concept of the unconscious. On the first count, that of being part of a new paradigm, this is obviously the case: here the unconscious makes an appearance in a quite different field of discourse and from rather different initial assumptions to those found in psychoanalysis. On the second, that it was discovered using methods of investigation quite different from those of Freud, the case is equally clear: the discovery of the dynamic unconscious by sociobiologists proceeds from rather different empirical and methodological approaches from those used by Freud. Finally, the third aspect, that the original discovery had been discounted or forgotten: as I argued at the very beginning, it is undeniable that, like Darwinism at the turn of the century, psychoanalysis has at best an insecure foothold among the modern sciences, and even though Freud's relevance is, as we have seen, explicitly recognized by some sociobiologists, it appears to be largely overlooked by others. Consequently, although I doubt very much whether any modern biologist would want to claim that this

new insight into the unconscious could be called revolutionary on a par with Einstein's rediscovery of the corpuscular
nature of light, I think that the case for regarding it as an
important discovery – albeit a *rediscovery* – is proved.

Parental investment and the causes of the Oedipus complex

However, the rediscovery of the unconscious is not the only
respect in which the researches of sociobiology in general and
Robert Trivers in particular have converged on the findings
of psychoanalysis. In one other important way they might be
seen to complement and vindicate what is perhaps, after the
discovery of the dynamic unconscious, the most characteristic finding of psychoanalysis: the dynamic and indeed conflicting interactions of parents and children in childhood
culminating in the central theorem of the psychoanalytic
view of development – the Oedipus complex.

In another well-known paper[20] Trivers applies Hamilton's
concept of inclusive fitness to the study of parent–offspring
conflict. Trivers begins by pointing out that once one aban-
dons the traditional limitation of only seeing parent–offspring relations from the point of view of the parent and
instead

> one imagines offspring as *actors* in this interaction, then con-
> flict must be assumed to lie at the heart of sexual reproduction
> itself – an offspring attempting from the very beginning to
> maximize its reproductive success would presumably want
> more investment than the parent is selected to give.[21]

An example of what he has in mind might be the case of
weaning. Here, it is not difficult to imagine that the interests
of the mother in providing milk and that of the offspring in

[20] R. Trivers, 'Parent–Offspring Conflict', *American Zoologist*, 14, 1974.
[21] Ibid., p. 249.

consuming it might clash, particularly if further provision might reduce the future reproductive success of the mother (even though it might promote that of the offspring).

Trivers remarks in his paper that

> the arguments presented here are particularly relevant to understanding a species such as the human species in which parental investment is critical to the offspring throughout its entire prereproductive life (and often later as well) and in which an individual normally spends its life embedded in a network of near and distant kin.[22]

He points out that an offspring, in competing with the parent for scarce resources which that parent might invest elsewhere, cannot rely on brute force, lacks experience and control of the resources at the command of mature individuals, and so generally competes at a disadvantage. This leads him to the conclusion that 'Given this competitive disadvantage, the offspring is expected to employ psychological rather than physical tactics.'[23] It will have to employ signals, such as cries, gestures or, in the case of human beings, facial expressions, in order to communicate its needs to the parent (and of course later, in the human case, will add words to its repertoire). Yet, as in the earlier discussion of reciprocal altruism, we must not make the mistake of naïvely imagining that animal communications are always communications of truth merely because it is hard to see how the communication of falsehoods could benefit the species.[24] On the contrary, taking the dynamic, authentically Darwinian view which sees evolution in terms of competition among individuals,

> The most important thing to realize about systems of animal communication is that they are not expected to be systems for the dissemination of truth. Instead, they are expected to be

[22] Ibid., p. 250.
[23] Ibid., p. 257.
[24] Trivers, 'Sociobiology and Politics', p. 34.

systems by which individual organisms attempt to maximize
their inclusive fitnesses by communicating to others things
that may be true or false.[25]

Thus we might expect to find all the deceptive phenomena
which we noticed in our discussion of the comparable cases
of reciprocal altruism: mimicry, misrepresentation, hypoc-
risy and various displays of sham emotion. Trivers also
suggests that we might find one further, unmistakably Freudian phenomenon, namely, *regression*.

Making a point which is particularly pertinent to the
human case, Trivers remarks that

> In those species in which the offspring is more helpless and
> vulnerable the younger it is, its parents will have been more
> strongly selected to respond positively to signals of need
> emitted by younger as opposed to older offspring. This sug-
> gests that at any stage of ontogeny in which the offspring is in
> conflict with its parents, one appropriate tactic may be to
> revert to the gestures and actions of an earlier stage of
> development in order to induce the investment that would
> have been forthcoming. Psychologists have long recognized
> such a tendency in humans and called it *regression*.[26]

Here, if Trivers had included references, they would have
been more-or-less exclusively Freudian in provenance and
would most certainly have overwhelmingly borne out his
conclusion. Clinical data, quite apart from personal experience, strongly argue for his case. Perhaps the ultimate ploy in
this respect – if we take intra-uterine existence to represent in
a certain sense maximal maternal provision – was demonstrated by a child of a colleague of mine who, when he
indicated to visitors that a sibling was growing inside his
mother, added 'And I'm getting in there as soon as he gets
out!' Certainly, everyday observation, quite apart from the
findings of the psychoanalysis of children, suggests that

[25] Ibid., p. 33.
[26] Ibid., p. 28.

stress, competition with other siblings and a need for increased parental investment in general will often trigger some regressive behaviour in children, and, as we shall see in a moment, this may be an important feature in explaining a unique feature of human anatomical, quite apart from psychological, evolution.

It may well be relevant to the present discussion to notice that, at the very beginning of the psychoanalytic revolution, when Freud was only just starting to develop the mature psychoanalytic method, he constantly found his patients reporting instances of childhood seduction by parents, nurses, servants and so on. Later, when he began to see the immense psychological significance of these early sexual experiences and when he had accumulated sufficient data on the subject, he realized that his patients were, in part at least, misrepresenting the truth. The discovery of the Oedipus complex – certainly Freud's most momentous discovery, apart from that of the unconscious in general – dates from the time when Freud began to realize that many of these stories of parental seduction were in large part false and that in effect they were (in a way which is typical of the dynamic unconscious) instances of *projection* – that is, phantasies[27] which shifted onto the parental figure motives which had in reality arisen in the child. In this way childhood sexuality was discovered and psychoanalytic investigations led Freud to the discovery of the Oedipus complex.

Although the fact of the existence of the Oedipus complex soon became clear in psychoanalysis and was corroborated by a vast amount of empirical data, the full reason for its existence has not been so obvious. Freud regarded it in large part as a consequence of the length of human childhood and the fact that sexual maturity was delayed until puberty. He saw the early efflorescence of childhood sexuality as a sort of archaeological vestige of a stage in evolution when sexual maturity occurred much earlier. As we shall see shortly, this

[27] Here I follow the psychoanalytic convention of spelling this word with a 'ph' when it refers to *unconscious* imagery.

view is certainly in part correct, but it is tempting to see infantile sexuality, not to mention the distortion, misrepresentation and sheer volume of forgetting which surrounds it, as a consequence of Trivers' general principle of parent–offspring conflict and as explicable in terms of its value to the child *as a potential means of parental seduction.* In other words, we might see infantile sexuality, in part at least (and perhaps in the most important part in so far as it affects the Oedipus complex), as motivated by the child's need to exploit not merely psychological tactics like those envisaged by Trivers, but psycho-sexual strategies like those uncovered by Freud.

We have already noted Trivers' suggestion that regression might serve to elicit greater parental response to the demands of the child. Yet regression is fundamentally a passive ploy in parent–offspring interaction: it tries to elicit greater investment by making the offspring appear even more dependent than usual. There seems no good reason why, if the child may adopt such a passive, regressive psychological tactic, it might not also adopt an active, precocious one when circumstances permit. Helplessness is not, after all, the only behaviour which will elicit a positive, supportive response from parents. Adults frequently use other ploys besides, such as those intended to arouse the interest and commitment of another by active means, such as showing an interest in them and making a prior commitment which will demand a compensating return. If adults can use these tactics in order to arouse the interests of others in themselves I see no reason why children should not do so too, at least when they are sufficiently mature to be able to exploit the repertoire of linguistic and emotional responses necessary to do so (something which experience teaches is not very old at all, and should certainly be seen in normal children by about the ages of four or five).

If an adult, particularly one of the opposite sex to the child, is the target of the advances, sexual interest may also play a part and an attempt to arouse sexual feelings may seem just as likely to benefit the instigator of the tactic as the arousal of any other kind of positive response. Indeed, given the strength, urgency and general lability of the sexual drive in human beings, exploiting it for this purpose may be especially effective.

The existence of paedophilia suggests that children, and even quite young ones, can be objects of sexual interest to some adults. Furthermore, given the diffuse nature of the sexual drive in human beings, and its tendency to underlie all manifestations of love and affection even within the family, it is not difficult to see how an active, precocious libidinal interest on the part of the child in the parents (and perhaps especially in the parent of the opposite sex) might serve to elicit greater investment and responsiveness from them, thereby promoting the fitness of the child and also providing a classical Darwinian foundation for the evolution, not only of childhood sexuality in general, but also of the Oedipus complex in particular. (It is certainly a fact that many of the behavioural manifestations of infantile sexuality during the Oedipal period (age 3-6) are exhibitionistic, seductive and seem designed to arouse the sexual interests of adults, as well as manifesting those of the child.)

If this were to be so, then it would also immediately follow that it would probably be in the best interests of the child to remain *unconscious* of the sexual element in its seductive precocity since, by employing sexual cues, especially directed at the parent of the opposite sex, it would implicitly run the risk of arousing the jealousy of the parent of the same sex. An active, sexually precocious seduction for the purposes of a greater maternal response might well serve the interests of the little boy, but not if it aroused jealousy and anger against him on the part of his father, whose protection, attention and general support we must presume the boy also needs. It might pay the child of either sex to dissimulate its active, libidinal advances behind a mask of playfulness, childishness and general psycho-sexual disingenuousness. If it came to direct sexual rivalry with the same-sex parent the child would obviously be at a great disadvantage and could not be expected to play an adult sexual role. Therefore its childhood one must be covert, unconscious to itself and preferably also to its parents, and generally dissimulated.

But if this were so it would only be because its rivalry was genuine, even if its sexual competence was not. The fact that it is greater parental investment rather than its own sexual satisfaction which the child attempts to secure in no way prevents it from seeing its same-sex parent as a rival if it is the libidinal element in its relationship with the opposite-sex parent which is being exploited. If this competition with the same-sex parent leads to typically childish wishes – that is, to wishes relatively independent of reality and unconstrained as to extent – then we might expect to find the typical, albeit usually repressed death-wishes against the father which accompany the Oedipal development of the little boy or the corresponding, if more complex, death-wishes against the mother which accompany that of the little girl.[28]

Furthermore, the widely-reported finding in psychoanalysis that such death-wishes are particularly potent in males may not merely reflect the greater simplicity of the male Oedipus complex and the greater aggressiveness usually found in that sex. It is possible that, thanks to a further prediction of the theory of parental investment,[29] human mothers might be behaviourally predisposed to invest preferentially in males if they were of high social status themselves or believed that their sons might be more effective than other males in reproducing the genes which they shared in common with them. This is because, thanks to the differential

[28] A delightful example of these wishes was once afforded by one of my own sons. Following a breakfast-table conversation not uncommon with four-year-old boys following on demands as to why he could not marry his mother etc., I was leaving the house some time later when he ran up and, obviously meaning to say 'Daddy, let me kiss you!' actually said 'Daddy, let me kill you!'

[29] R. Trivers and D. Willard, 'Natural Selection of Parental Ability to Vary the Sex Ratio of Offspring', *Science*, 179, 1973, pp. 90–2.

nature of each sex's investment in its gametes, males can usually leave many more offspring than can females (as David Barash points out, where Queen Hecuba of Troy was said to have had 20 children, King Ismail of Morocco is reported to have fathered 1056![30]).

If both sons and daughters deploy Oedipal cues in trying to solicit greater parental investment it is possible not only that boys will tend to target the mother both early and later but that those who were particularly effective in displaying Oedipal behaviour might be unconsciously preferred by mothers, who would see such childhood sexual precocity as evidence of future adult sexual precociousness and reproductive success. Signs of aggressiveness displayed against the father in this situation might also then be interpreted unconsciously by mothers as evidence of superior Darwinian fitness in their sons since much individual reproductive success in adult life involves competition with other males for access to females. In this way, childhood Oedipal dramas might evolve as unconscious prefigurements of later sexual conflicts, an observation which might to some very considerable extent explain not only their evolutionary foundation in the latent fitness-maximizing possibilities of the human family, but also some of the immense significance which these childhood anticipations of sexual life seem to have for adults.

(Whatever the truth of these conjectures, it is undeniable that Sigmund Freud enjoyed considerable preference where parental investment was concerned over his sisters, and there is no doubt that he regarded the preference shown to him by his mother in particular as one of the most important factors in promoting his own success in life: 'A man who has been the undisputed favourite of his mother keeps for life the feeling of being a conqueror, that confidence of success that so often induces real success.'[31] How far such a feeling of having successfully exploited what we might call the Oedipal ploy in human parent–offspring conflict contributed to Freud

[30] Barash, *Sociobiology and Behaviour*, p. 224.
[31] E. Jones, *The Life and Work of Sigmund Freud*, vol. 1, p. 5.

discovering the Oedipus complex we shall perhaps never know, but the facts suggest that the connection might not be entirely accidental.)

In summary then, it begins to seem as if the theory of parent–offspring conflict, as applied to our own species with all its manifold complexities of behaviour, psychology and response, might – if we were not too easily put off by the very dissimulations of the truth which the theory predicts – tempt us to conclude that all the features of the classical Freudian Oedipus complex were entirely to be expected: the precocious, active libidinal development in early childhood; the tendency for both sexes originally to direct their attention to the mother but later to target the parent of the opposite sex; the tendency to see the same-sex parent as a feared rival, to resent their competition and to harbour death-wishes against them; the tendency for the whole complex to be especially strongly developed in males; finally, the inclination to repress the whole phenomenon and safeguard it from conscious awareness, perhaps even to the point of maintaining the fiction of infantile innocence and manifesting resistance to any theory such as Freud's which threatened to undo the whole defence and allow the return of the repressed to consciousness.

Such a theory of childhood sexuality would immediately complement many findings of psychoanalysis. For instance, it would provide a very satisfyingly basic explanation for the widely observed fact that Oedipal conflicts are often exacerbated in children who have received too little or too much parental investment – those with too little are presumably exaggerating a normal strategy which had failed at normal levels of application and those with too much are perhaps exploiting a winning tactical advantage. Again, it would transparently explain the complication of dependency which accompanies excessive Oedipal involvements, particularly in adolescence (and which is an important factor in understanding modern societies, as we shall see in a later chapter). Above all, it would provide a sound biological basis for one of the most important findings of psychoanalysis and would serve to do much to counteract one of the most serious drawbacks of the sociobiological approach as applied to human beings, namely, its tendency, despite its rediscovery of an authentically Darwinian, dynamic biological approach, to discount dynamic psychology.

Parent-child conflict and the incest-taboo

One of the best examples of this failing, and certainly the most crucial case as far as an understanding of human societies is concerned, is the tendency of sociobiologists to assume that incest-avoidance is in some relatively straightforward way genetically determined. Of course, if this were the case, then the Oedipus complex would have to be what many clearly wish it were – a figment of Freud's imagination. That it is no such thing is painfully obvious to anyone who has ever undergone a competently carried out classical analysis or has taken the trouble to consult the now vast psychoanalytic literature. But empirical refutation of the naïve biological theory is not our concern here.[32] What I want to point out is that Trivers' theory of parent–offspring conflict, if applied to the findings of psychoanalysis regarding the Oedipus complex as I am suggesting here, provides a satisfying and biologically and psychologically sound explanation of why children may be motivated by their evolutionary self-interest to manifest seductive sexual advances towards parental figures (most successfully, of course, to those of the opposite sex), and why parents might be correspondingly motivated to oppose such seductions and to attempt to counter them with their own psychological weapons, one of the most effective of which is the incest-prohibition.

[32] See M. E. Spiro's *Oedipus in the Trobriands*, chapter 6 for a critique of the sparse and ambiguous empirical evidence on which the naïve biological-determinist theory of incest-avoidance is based.

The fundamental objection to the naïve biological theory of human incest-avoidance, quite apart from the overwhelming empirical difficulties involved in explaining away the frequency of incest, the necessity of cultural prohibitions if we already possess genetic determinations against it and so on, lies in the fact that it is essentially non-dynamic. In time, it may well come to be seen as a vestige of the old species-advantage reasoning which assumes that incest is 'bad for the species'.[33] Of course, as biologists like Trivers would be the first to point out, the same applies to all kinds of conflict (even parent–offspring conflict perhaps), but that does not prevent conflict being one of the fundamental realities in the existence of most organisms. As a non-dynamic, fundamentally euphemistic idea it assumes that human behaviour is in this instance under automatic biological control which makes humans not normally interested in incest and in some unspecified way brings cultural factors, such as incest-taboos and elaborate kinship systems, into being to bolster this aversion (without explaining why it should need bolstering if efficiently genetically determined in the first place).

The assumption that human beings are passively prevailed upon by their genes to want to avoid sexual contact with close kin is not only wildly at variance with the facts as recorded in literally thousands upon thousands of cases of psychoanalysis (not to mention criminal investigations into multitudinous cases of incest, child-molestation and sexual assault); it also, from the theoretical point of view, repeats the fundamental error of the holistic school of social thought which sees the individual as a passive subject before the irresistible determining force of his culture. So widely disseminated did this view become and so effective a hold did it have on most people earlier in this century that even the

---

[33] For instance, M. Ruse and E. O. Wilson state that 'Ethical codes work because they drive us to go against our selfish day-to-day impulses *in favour of long-term group survival and harmony*' (my italics). Earlier they specify 'the avoidance of incest' as one of the ethical codes they have in mind. ('The Evolution of Ethics'. *New Scientist*, 17 Oct. 1985.)

pioneers of psychoanalysis at first made the error of over-estimating the efficacy of education and indoctrination. Commenting on early optimism in the psychoanalytic movement about enlightened child-rearing and the good effects it was expected to have, Anna Freud reveals that

> It was unexpected that even the most well-meant and simply worded sexual enlightenment was not readily acceptable to young children and that they persisted in clinging to what had to be recognized as their own sexual theories which translate adult genitality into the age-appropriate terms of orality, violence and mutilation . . . Above all, to rid the child of anxiety proved an impossible task. Parents did their best to reduce the children's fear of them, merely to find that they were increasing guilt feelings, i.e., fears of the child's own conscience.[34]

In a related context, Anna Freud was fond of quoting the example of young Jewish children who, during the Nazi persecution in Germany, were often to be seen – much to the consternation of their parents – marching up and down, giving fascist salutes and generally playing at being storm-troopers. Unless we are expected to believe that National Socialist ideology or anti-Semitic Germanic social consciousness was a more powerful socializing force than the Jewish children's own parental culture – an unlikely proposition if there ever was one – we can only conclude, as Anna Freud did, that here we have an example of a well-known psychological defence on the part of young children: identification with the aggressor. In short, what we have is a *dynamic* response to an unbearable situation, one which turns a latent psychological factor – fear of the aggressor – into its manifest opposite – identification with him – for purely defensive purposes. Here, indeed, we have a characteristically human and, it must be admitted, characteristically perverse response.

[34] Anna Freud, *Normality and Pathology in Childhood*, pp. 7–8.

I would suggest that the conclusion to be drawn from the dynamic biological approach of writers like Hamilton and Trivers, particularly if we are considering the latter's theory of parent–offspring conflict as applied to human beings, is that it requires a natural complement in a dynamic psychology, not one which naïvely assumes a simple, direct and one-way communication between genes and behaviour. If we restrict ourselves for the time being just to children, in whom, one would have thought, elemental human proclivities should be most clearly obvious, we find the perplexing, perverse picture we noticed above in connection with defences against aggression. Speaking in general of dispositions found in children, Anna Freud says that

> There are *shyness* and *modesty* which are reaction formations and as such complete reversals of former exhibitionistic tendencies; there is, further, the behaviour commonly described as *buffoonery* or *clowning* which, in analysis, has been revealed as a distortion of phallic exhibitionism, with the showing off displaced from an asset of the individual to one of his defects. *Exaggerated manliness* and *noisy aggression* are overcompensations which betray underlying castration fears. Complaints about being *maltreated* and *discriminated against* are a transparent defence against passive fantasies and wishes.[35]

In passages like this we find the empirical validation for Trivers' expectation that 'from an early age the offspring is expected to be a psychologically sophisticated organism.'[36] Furthermore, we find precisely the sort of distortion, reversal and mimicking which his theory of dynamic interactions between parent and offspring have led us to expect. We see examples of reaction-formations, which disguise the truth by turning it into its opposite; we see over-compensations which serve to hide the truth by sheer stridency of protestation; we see the expression of wishes whose manifest content serves to hide an altogether different but latent one.

[35] Ibid., pp. 18–19 (Anna Freud's italics).
[36] Trivers, 'Sociobiology and Politics', p. 29.

Far from being peculiar to childhood, it seems that such perverse distortions of the psychological and biological truth are absolutely typical of human beings and the hall-mark of their culture. But let us return to the Oedipus complex for a moment and look at it from the other side of the picture – that of the parent.

Trivers' approach, like the psychoanalytic one, leads him to conclude that 'it is clearly a mistake to view socialization in humans as only, or even primarily, a process of 'enculturation' by which parents teach their offspring their culture.'[37] He begins by pointing out that, according to Hamilton's concept of inclusive fitness, an individual is only expected to perform an altruistic act towards a full-sibling if the benefit to the sibling is greater than twice the cost to the altruist. This is because the full-sibling has, on average, half the same genes as the altruist. By similar argument, selfish acts whose cost falls on a full-sibling will be avoided only when their cost exceeds twice their benefit to the actor. Nevertheless, parents, who are equally related to all their offspring, will take a different view of the matter. They will tend to encourage all altruistic acts among their offspring whose benefit is greater than their cost and similarly to discourage all selfish acts whose cost is greater than their benefit. For instance, offspring will only be selected to perform altruistic acts for cousins related through the mother if the benefit is eight times the cost (since only one-eighth of the altruist's genes are found in his cousins); but, since the mother is more closely related to her nephews and nieces, she would like to see altruistic acts performed whenever benefit is twice the cost. Trivers concludes:

> As it applies to human beings, the preceding argument can be summarized by saying that a fundamental conflict is expected during socialization over the altruistic and egoistic impulses of the offspring. Parents are expected to socialize their offspring to act more altruistically and less egoistically than the offspring would naturally act, and the offspring are expected

[37] Ibid., p. 33.

to resist such socialization . . . According to the theory presented here, socialization is a process by which parents attempt to mold each offspring in order to increase their own inclusive fitness, whereas each offspring is selected to resist some of the molding and to attempt to mold the behaviour of its parents (and siblings) in order to increase its own inclusive fitness.[38]

If we assume, as I have done here, that infantile sexuality is a manifestation of such an attempted moulding of the parental behaviour by the child, then we can go some way beyond the earlier psychoanalytic theory of the Oedipus complex and agree with Trivers that

> Conflict during socialization need not be viewed solely as conflict between the culture of the parent and the biology of the child.[39]

On the contrary, we can now see that it is based in the biology of both parties, but that it is in the biological interests of the parents, quite apart from their cultural or psychological interests, to sustain a role which demands greater moral self-sacrifice than the young may wish to give and to discourage more selfish behaviour than the young would wish to be discouraged from performing. Indeed,

> Since teaching (as opposed to molding) is expected to be recognized by offspring as being in their own self-interest, parents would be expected to overemphasize their role as teachers in order to minimize resistance in their young. According to this view, then, the prevailing concept of socialization is to some extent a view that one would expect adults to entertain and disseminate.[40]

Indeed, we could go further and say that holistic, cultural-determinist theories of socialization which see the child as a

[38] Ibid., p. 32.
[39] Ibid., p. 32.
[40] Ibid., p. 32.

largely passive recipient of cultural conditioning only consider what Trivers here calls 'moulding', and that, in doing so, they inherently adopt an authoritarian, parental and completely one-sided view of socialization.

Paradoxically enough, so does the naïve biological-determinist view of the incest-taboo. If we accept that human offspring use psycho-sexual as well as just purely psychological weapons in their attempt to mould parental behaviour and that, in accordance with observation, both sexes might try this first on the most important figure in early childhood – the mother – but might later find it most effective with the parent of the opposite sex (thereby explaining some of the peculiarities of the female Oedipus complex), we ought also to point out that Trivers' theory suggests that it will be to some extent in the parents' own biological self-interest to resist and to prevent the child making demands in terms of parental investment which go beyond what the parents might wish to provide. As a consequence, the parents have an excellent motive not merely to resist seduction but to get the child to cooperate with the parental interest, which, we assume, usually stops far short of the amount of investment which the young might wish.

Indeed, things might go further than this since, as we saw when discussing Hamilton's theory of kin altruism, there may be situations in which individuals might increase their inclusive fitness by not reproducing. An obvious one which springs to mind is that where, because an individual is related to its siblings to the same extent that it is to its own offspring (by half its genes), it might, in certain circumstances, pay an individual to look after its brothers and sisters rather than raise young of its own if by so doing more of its genes would be represented in the next generation. If we accept this – and we saw earlier that this, essentially, is the explanation of the altruism of the social insects – then it follows that it is even more likely that by not reproducing in their own right some individuals might increase their *parents'* inclusive fitness more than they might their own. In these circumstances it might pay parents to try to prevent some of their offspring reproducing altogether and, in those situations where the offspring's own inclusive fitness was lowered by this stratagem, Trivers speculates that the individual concerned might be

> expected to show internal conflict over its adult role and to express ambivalence over the past, particularly over the behaviour of its parents . . . It remains to be explored to what extent the etiology of sexual preferences (such as homosexuality) which tend to interfere with reproduction can be explained in terms of the present argument.[41]

Here again, the Freudian overtones are unmistakable, especially with the mention of the word 'ambivalence' which, although coined by Bleuler, soon became current in psychoanalysis. Since ambivalence over the past role of the parents seems to be one of the central themes – if not *the* central theme – of human psychology the world over, and since, as we know, the etiology of sexual preferences is profoundly influenced by the experiences of early childhood and the whole performance of adult sexuality heavily indebted to oral, anal and phallic currents from infancy, it follows that parental moulding of childrens' sexual preferences is bound to be a major factor in human psychology, not merely in cases of homosexuality.

Here the incest-prohibition, along with general sexual taboos, particularly those affecting young children, might be expected to be an example of parental moulding masquerading as 'education' – moral education which claims that good little boys and girls do not think like that, do not want to behave like that, that incest is 'unnatural', not in the child's best interests, and so on. As Trivers points out, 'deception seems a natural ally of parental domination':

> A parent will minimize resistance in its offspring if it can convince the offspring that it is acting in the offspring's best

[41] Trivers, 'Parent–Offspring Conflict', p. 26

interest when, in fact, it is merely expressing its own self-interest. Any strategy of parental manipulation that is unfair must, in turn, be represented as fair even if the parent admits that it is not acting with only the offspring's self-interest in mind.[42]

Furthermore, the parents' repression of their own Oedipus complexes might be adaptive here. Since, as we shall see in the next chapter, identification seems to be the chief psychological mechanism by means of which kin altruism expresses itself in human behaviour and since parents inevitably need to identify with their offspring in order to mobilize such altruism as is involved in child-rearing, it follows that a tendency to remember themselves as having been innocent in their own childhoods will make it all the easier for parents to insist that their children should be correspondingly innocent in theirs. This in turn will only make it all the more important for children to hide Oedipal motivations which might tend to weaken parental identification with them and thereby endanger the basic kin altruism which underlies parental investment and child-rearing in general:

> The offspring is in an awkward position in such situations. On the one hand it is selected to resist parental domination; on the other hand such resistance may merely engender harsher parental maneuvers. Thus, the child may be selected to acquiesce in parental domination and to express toward the parent the affection and good spirit that the parent desires. This conflict may most easily be handled by rendering negative feelings towards the parent unconscious. Thus, we also expect *self-deception* in these interactions, rendering some facts unconscious on both sides the better to deceive others.[43]

If the general drift of my argument is correct – and it is hard to see how it cannot be once we accept that sexual

[42] Trivers, *Social Evolution*, p. 165.
[43] Ibid., p. 165.

factors might play the part they evidently do in parent–offspring interactions in our species – it is difficult not to see biological theories which deny the transparent incestuous element in infantile sexuality as doing anything other than perpetuating the parental myths and reinforcing a complacent, non-dynamic view which sees cultural prohibitions performing those naïvely truth-carrying, informative roles which all communications were once supposed to perform. Much more plausible is it to suggest, as Freud did, that the very existence of a taboo against incest proves its attraction to human beings and that the facts of infantile sexuality, the family setting and the inevitable conflict to be expected between sons and fathers, mothers and daughters, means that here, as elsewhere, cultural prohibitions do not passively repeat the urgings of nature, but react against them with typical, dynamic and perverse effects.

It seems increasingly clear that both Freudians and Darwinists can now agree that

> *The personality and conscience of the child is formed in an arena of conflict.* Since the personality and conscience of a child is expected to affect the child's altruism and selfishness, these characteristics may be a matter of disagreement between parent and offspring. So far as we know, personality and conscience are formed early in socialization, probably during the first five years of a child's life. We expect the child to develop during this time internal representations of its parents' viewpoints as well as its own. These may be in conflict, requiring mediation by a third entity. This suggests a similarity to Freud's system of id, superego and ego. The *id* represents the internal, innate, egoistic impulses of the Freudian system. We might say it represents the offspring's own self-interest. The *superego* represents the internalized demands of the parents and is developed in interactions with them. The *ego*, in turn, acts as a referee, reconciling the demands of the id and the superego.[44]

[44] Ibid., p. 163 (Trivers' emphasis). For a fuller discussion of the relations between Freud's id-ego-superego paradigm and sociobiology and a suggested reformulation see below pp. 165–71.

Thus spoke Sigmund Freud

In summarizing and drawing together the various strands of this discussion let me revert to the earlier point about regression.

We saw that Trivers argued that since younger offspring usually require more parental investment than older ones a regression to earlier modes of behaviour may succeed in eliciting a greater degree of parental response to the needs of the offspring than otherwise. But there are good reasons for thinking that such a tendency to regression is not limited to the psychological sphere, but may also apply more widely.

In his comments on human reciprocal altruism, Trivers assumes that during the Pleistocene hominid societies were constituted on the popular chimpanzee model of social structure.[45] However that may be, the discovery by Clifford Jolly[46] of the remarkable and hitherto largely unnoticed parallels between hominid evolution and that of the modern gelada baboon indicates that what we may call the 'baboon model' has much to be said for it.

If we join Darwin,[47] Freud,[48] Fox,[49] Crook,[50] Jolly[51] and others in postulating a baboon model for the origins of hominid social structure we can see that little scope exists originally for the evolution of reciprocal altruism. According to the baboon – or, perhaps it would be more accurate to say, *gelada* baboon – model, human society originated in a social structure characterized by two kinds of group: so-called 'one-male groups' comprising a single dominant male and his harem and young, and 'all-male groups' consisting of young but sexually mature males and perhaps some older single males. In the latter, 'all-male' groups, reciprocal altruism

---

[45] Trivers, 'Sociobiology and Politics', pp. 10–11.
[46] C. Jolly, 'The Seed-Eaters: A New Model of Hominid Differentiation Based on a Baboon Analogy', *Man*, 5, 1970, pp. 5–27.
[47] C. Darwin, *The Descent of Man*.
[48] S. Freud, *Totem and Taboo*, XIII, pp. 140–6.
[49] R. Fox, *The Red Lamp of Incest*.
[50] J. H. Crook, *The Evolution of Human Consciousness*.
[51] Jolly, 'The Seed-Eaters'.

might have had much more opportunity to evolve than elsewhere, particularly when some of those groups began to experiment with cooperative big-game hunting. The cooperation this necessitated, the absence of females to motivate intra-group conflict and the move away from the independent food-gathering habits of vegetarian foraging all meant that young male hunting hominids were likely to have been the ones to take the first fateful steps towards the elaborate development of reciprocal altruism which has characterized human social evolution ever since.

In the original baboon-style social structure parent–offspring conflict produced exclusion of newly sexually mature males when fathers banished their sons from the group. With the beginnings of hunting, some bands of hunter sons may have maximized their inclusive fitness by taking females from the fathers in such a way that they maintained their reciprocal, altruistic relationships.[52] The crucial element here would have been sexual rivalry since it was this which would normally mean that any male in possession of a group of females would do his best to drive out rivals and remain in sole possession – to the obvious benefit of his genes. The immense adaptive advantages of cooperative hunting explain why it might be more profitable for a group of males to maintain their cooperation even after the acquisition of females rather than see their hunting band break up in internecine strife and the victor among them perforce return to vegetarian foraging (since females and young could not have been expected to participate in a communal hunt and could not have been left unguarded while the lone male did so, even assuming that he had much chance of success alone, which he would not have done).

In this scenario of human cultural evolution parent–offspring conflict takes a new turn: instead of being a question of individual father–son conflicts resulting in sons replacing fathers in their command of 'one-male' groups, entire groups of sons substitute themselves for the father and divide up the

[52] C. Badcock, *The Psychoanalysis of Culture*, pp. 12–28.

females among them in a more equitable way. Here a principal focus of repression – the need to deceive oneself in the interests of deceiving others – would have related to the question of sexual rivalry. Those groups whose members successfully hid the reality of their desires for sexual hegemony from themselves and their colleagues would have been those with the greatest chance of actually avoiding outbreaks of violence motivated by rivalry. If this were so then here would be the evolutionary origin of the incest-taboo, one nicely complementing the ontological theory relating it to parental investment set out earlier and adding to the latter's emphasis on the parent–child prohibition a complementary one on the brother–sister taboo.

At the same time, the new conditions of life would have favoured not merely the evolution of repression of sexual rivalry through the institution of incest-taboos but also what seems to have been the most important trend in recent human evolution, what is termed *foetalization* or *neoteny* – that is, a long-term evolutionary tendency towards increasing apparent immaturity in the adult form of the species. In its principal effect of providing adult human beings with the preponderance of brain over body development found otherwise only in the infantile forms of their predecessors, neoteny would have promoted the very neuro-anatomical requirements for repression and that general developmental plasticity which Trivers postulates as expectable in the circumstances.[53]

Yet there seems no way of reconciling the baboon model of social structure with neoteny since, in the first place, the modern gelada baboon shows not the slightest evidence of it and, in the second, it is almost impossible in principle to imagine how such a tendency in evolution could emerge in a social structure in which young males are expelled from the natal 'one-male group' at puberty and then usually have to challenge dominant males for the possession of females who otherwise remain their elders' exclusive possession. Since

[53] Trivers, 'Sociobiology and Politics'.

neoteny is a process whereby development is delayed to the extent that individuals come to resemble in their maturity the immature or even, in the human case, the unborn forms of their ancestors, it is difficult indeed to see how such a retardation in development could be advantageous to a gelada-like hominid. Furthermore, the principal effect of neoteny on the young of our species has been to make them increasingly dependent on parental care, something which is hard to reconcile with the life-style of a gelada-like forager which must spend nearly all its time on the move or gathering food.

Nevertheless, even though neoteny may not be explicable in gelada-like conditions, it is not at all difficult to see how it might be adaptive for early hominid hunters who would have doubtless been able to tolerate lengthy parental care because of the possibility of sharing their highly nutritious food-supply and of easily transporting it to home bases where mothers and young could remain. In these conditions it is easy to imagine that a generalized tendency to regression, not merely a psychological one, might have been in the interests of the young who would thereby have elicited considerably greater parental investment than would previously have been possible. Furthermore, the new conditions would have meant that such an investment might not have been disadvantageous for the parents since in a hunting economy the other consequences of neoteny – a lengthened period of educability in childhood and an absolute increase in brain/body weight ratio – would have been highly adaptive, given that hominid hunting had to rely on acquired cunning and technology, rather than on inherited dentition, brute force or fleetness of foot.

In short, neoteny, which is in some ways such a puzzling evolutionary tendency because of its general foetalizing effects, nevertheless finds a natural and intelligible basis in Trivers' theory of parent–offspring conflict. It also fits in nicely with the modern Freudian theory of the origin of culture because it leads in a similar natural and inevitable way to the understanding of the evolutionary origins of the

Oedipus complex and, if we include Trivers' general theory of reciprocal altruism, to an understanding of the evolution of the dynamic unconscious.[54]

Finally, in the new situation where prolonged parental care was adaptive, the individual origins of the Oedipus complex could be found so that infantile as well as adult sexual rivalry was progressively subjected to repression. In this way both the reciprocal altruism of the first hunter–gatherers, and the parent–offspring conflicts of those primal societies, conspired to promote what is perhaps the most prominent feature of human nature: its dynamic, topographical quality which renders whole regions of the mind unconscious and the whole stretch of early childhood not remembered at all or only fitfully recalled through a deep haze of forgetting. The repression of early childhood, like the exactly analogous need to repress contemporary realities, did not appear by accident. On the contrary, it was deeply motivated – indeed, it was selected by evolutionary forces which determined that hence-forth repression would be a major feature of human psychology and the unconscious the chief constituent of the mind.

The general conclusion that 'Freud's view is entirely compatible with sociobiological thinking', albeit made in a book whose subtitle, *The Whisperings Within*, might suggest that it was by a psychoanalyst, is in fact the judgement of David Barash[55] and it is one which, despite the differences which still remain between psychoanalysis and sociobiology, seems overwhelmingly justified. Once Darwinism was purged of most of its holistic contaminations and the modern theory of altruism began to be elaborated, it was inevitable that sooner or later evolutionary research would begin to uncover what had, in the event, already become apparent to psychoanalysis and that sociobiologists should rediscover those hidden, yet fundamental realities of which it could only be said: thus spoke Sigmund Freud.

[54] For a fuller account see Badcock, *The Psychoanalysis of Culture*, pp. 39–49.

[55] D. Barash, *Sociobiology: The Whisperings Within*, p. 213.

2

Kin Altruism, Identification and Masochism

Altruism-through-identification

Quite apart from the phenomenon of convergence on key psychoanalytic concepts such as the dynamic unconscious and the parent–offspring conflict which we call the Oedipus complex, modern Darwinism and Freudianism agree on one even more fundamental point – what we might term *the nullity of the subjective concept of altruism*.

In the case of biology it is easy to understand why a subjective definition of altruism would not do: we simply cannot attribute subjective intentions to animals even when, as in the case of the social insects, their behaviour appears to be archetypically altruistic. There is an understandable desire to try to define such self-sacrificing behaviour in objective rather than subjective terms, and so we have little choice but to conclude that the term 'altruism' can only be ascribed to animal behaviour in circumstances where one organism promotes the fitness of another at its own expense. Since the definition of 'fitness' here is the Darwinian one which speaks purely in terms of reproductive success, it follows that ideal altruism – that is, altruism defined in subjective, human terms – cannot be expected to evolve.

However we look at it, such alleged pure altruism is a profound problem for evolutionary theory, suggesting either that evolution cannot explain it, or that, if it can, some way must be found to show how such an apparently paradoxical and self-defeating behaviour could become established. As far as the human case is concerned, it is obvious that if we wish to go beyond the purely objective definition of altruism outlined above and make a special case for human intentions as definitive of pure altruism, everything turns on the validity of the case which can be made out for such subjective altruistic intentions.

The classic discussion of altruism in psychoanalysis occurs in Anna Freud's *The Ego and the Mechanisms of Defence*. Speaking of the problem many years later she remarked that, far from being born altruistic, or even becoming altruistic out of the goodness of their hearts, human beings are good '*out of the badness of (their) hearts*'.[1]

In her book Anna Freud showed how apparent acts of selfless devotion to others – ideal altruism if it ever existed – were found to be, on analysis, rather less altruistic than they seemed. A key psychological mechanism turned out to be *identification*. She gives an example of a young governess whom she analysed who was notable for

> her unassuming character and the modesty of her demands on life . . . she was unmarried and childless and rather shabby and inconspicuous. She showed little sign of envy or ambition . . . The repudiation of her own sexuality did not prevent her from taking an affectionate interest in the love life of her women friends and colleagues. She was an enthusiastic match-maker and many love affairs were confided to her. Although she took no trouble with her own dress, she displayed a lively interest in her friends' clothes. Childless herself, she was devoted to other people's children . . . Instead of exerting herself to achieve any aims of her own, she expended all her energy in sympathizing with the experiences of people she cared for.[2]

But this impressive display of altruism turned out to be selfishly motivated when the analysis revealed that

[1] Anna Freud in conversation with Joseph Sandler, recorded in *Bulletin of the Hampstead Clinic*, 6, 1983, p. 332. My italics.
[2] A. Freud, *The Ego and the Mechanisms of Defence*, pp. 124–5.

The vanity of her women friends provided, as it were, a foothold for the projection of her own vanity, while her libidinal wishes and ambitious fantasies were likewise deposited in the outside world. She projected her prohibited instinctual impulses onto other people . . . The patient did not dissociate herself from her proxies but identified herself with them. She showed her sympathy with their wishes and felt that there was an extraordinarily strong bond between these people and herself . . . She gratified her instincts by sharing in the gratification of others, employing for this purpose the mechanisms of projection and identification . . . The surrender of her instinctual impulses in favour of other people had thus an egoistic significance, but in her efforts to gratify the impulses of others her behaviour could only be called altruistic.[3]

Speaking in general Anna Freud adds that

Any number of cases similar to those which I have quoted can be observed in everyday life . . . For instance, a young girl, who had scruples of conscience about marrying herself, did all she could to encourage her sister's engagement. A patient, who suffered from obsessional inhibitions in spending any money on herself, had no hesitation in spending lavishly on presents. Another patient, who was prevented by anxiety from carrying out her plans for travel, was quite unexpectedly pressing in her advice to her friends to do so.[4]

Altruism-through-identification need not only be benign, it can draw on aggressive drives as well:

Perhaps the most extreme instance is that of the assassin who, in the name of the oppressed, murders the oppressor. The object against which the liberated aggression is directed is invariably the representative of the authority which imposed renunciation of instinct on the subject in infancy.[5]

But perhaps the most common – and certainly, the most normal – example of altruism-through-identification is found

[3] Ibid., p. 126.
[4] Ibid., pp. 128–9.
[5] Ibid., p. 130.

within the family, and in the common tendency for parents to identify with their children:

> We know that parents sometimes delegate to their children their projects for their own lives, in a manner at once altruistic and egoistic. It is as if they hoped through the child, whom they regard as better qualified for the purpose than themselves, to wrest from life the fulfilment of the ambitions which they themselves have failed to realize. Perhaps even the purely altruistic relation of a mother to her son is largely determined by such a surrender of her own wishes to the object whose sex makes him 'better qualified' to carry them out. A man's success in life does, indeed, go far to compensate the women of his family for the renunciation of their own ambitions.[6]

These observations suggest an interesting equation of the typically human phenomenon of altruism-through-identification with kin altruism because in both cases we have altruism which is explicable through an essential identity – an objective genetic identity in the biological instance and a subjective, psychological identity in the other. Indeed, far from being a purely formal resemblance, such instances of altruism-through-identification may well be the means by which human beings are predisposed to manifest what biologists would call kin altruism, since it is hard to see how such a common psychological phenomenon could exist without some innate behavioural predisposition towards it.

Looked at from this point of view, Anna Freud's mention of the altruistic identification of a mother with her son provides a possible psychological mechanism whereby the human equivalent of kin altruism might come about. It certainly does not seem far-fetched to suppose that some basic genetic programming might exist which predisposes individuals to be more likely to act altruistically towards others who remind them of themselves in some way or another – especially since such resemblances, whether of physical appearance, psychology or behaviour, would doubtless have been based on shared heredity in the small,

[6] Ibid., pp. 131–2.

dispersed groups in which our hominid ancestors probably lived and in which any such genetically-determined traits would have had to become established.

If the mechanism of identification does operate like this then it is easy to see it as a human, psychological equivalent of what is often called *phenotypic matching* in biology: that is, using oneself as a model for comparison with others:

> genes do not recognize themselves directly in other creatures, but rather, in many animal species, individuals are able to measure relatedness by learning some standard of comparison, such as the self, by which others are then discriminated.[7]

If this suggestion is correct then here we have the dynamic, psychological means by which much of what we might have classified as kin altruism in primal societies may have come about. By means of identifications and projections like those discussed above individuals may have been dynamically motivated to act altruistically towards those to whom in the conditions of primal societies they would have been most likely to have been related. In this way the degree of subjective identification may well have reflected the degree of objective relatedness and may have correlated positively with the extent to which one individual's self-love could have been projected onto another to whom they were related. As a consequence of such a tendency to identify, narcissism, otherwise presumably adapted solely to serve the self-preserving interests of the individual, could have been extended by projection to serve the interests of the genes which identifiable individuals could have been assumed to hold in common.

The use of the self as a standard of comparison for judging relatedness would explain the otherwise perplexing process whereby the narcissism of the self could become deployed in the altruistic interests of others. It would reveal the unconscious – ultimately genetic – self-interest which belies the otherwise apparently disinterested appearance of much

[7] R. Trivers, *Social Evolution*, p. 134.

human altruism and provide a satisfying evolutionary foundation for the purely psychological observations of altruism-through-identification quoted above.

Altruism and masochism

The concept of identification, although powerful in explaining much altruistic behaviour in modern human beings, must not be taken to apply only to conscious, common-sense identifications, or even to straightforward unconscious ones. Whilst it is certainly the case that the facts of modern life mean that individuals encounter, and have the opportunity to form identifications with, a vast number of people to whom they are probably not at all closely related, thereby extending the psychological mechanisms on which primal kin altruism depends to new and biologically unforeseen applications (some more of which we will review later), it is nevertheless important to realize that even in relations with close kin identification does not necessarily come about in a simple or straightforward way and may easily lead to apparently perverse and complex results.

Some of the most puzzling of these – and some, furthermore, which superficially seem to give most credence to the idea of pure altruism in human beings – are explicable as consequences of those forms of identification which give rise to *masochism*.

Because all definitions agree that altruism involves self-sacrifice, and because all self-sacrifice must be injurious in some way to the self in order to be genuinely self-sacrificial, the psychological equation 'altruism equals masochism' follows directly as a consequence of whatever definition of altruism we adopt, objective or subjective. In this way the self-injuring aspect of pure altruism which underlies its impossibility in evolutionary terms surfaces again as a paradox in psychological terms: 'real' altruists act by definition against their own personal self-interest, or, at least, so it seems if their claims to ideal altruism are to be believed.

Yet even though self-sacrifice is injurious, it is not inexplicable in psychoanalytic terms. On the contrary, examples of it abound from self-injuring Freudian slips and mistakes to the more bizarre forms of masochistic sexual perversion. In the dynamic, conflicting interplay of psychological forces which is distinctive of the psychoanalytic view of human psychology and which so characteristically distinguishes it from the static approach of the academic schools, masochism is only one of many instances where psychological currents originally mobilized to give more straightforward gratifications eventually come to give more perverse and indirect ones.

Since masochism is pleasurable to masochists, ideal, self-sacrificing altruism can indeed reward the person who practises it. Indeed, when we examine the historical record of the more spectacular instances of masochistic altruism such as those, for instance, found in the history of religion, we cannot help noticing that very often those who lived lives of exemplary self-sacrifice also frequently found the need to practise mortifications of their bodies as likely to appear in the novels of Sacher-Masoch as in works of hagiography. Yet masochism need not only be erotic. In a famous paper on the subject,[8] Freud defined two other kinds, one being what he termed 'moral masochism' and which, in its highly ethical, idealized and sublimated manifestation of self-punishment provides the principal dynamic psychological foundation for masochistic altruism. By inflicting purely psychological punishments on himself the moral masochist is likely to welcome every instance of failure, injustice, cruelty, derision and unhappiness that he suffers as fulfilments of his deepest need:

> The suffering itself is what matters . . . It may even be caused by impersonal powers or by circumstances; the true masochist always turns his cheek whenever he has a chance of receiving a blow.[9]

[8] S. Freud, 'The Economic Problem of Masochism', XIX, pp. 159–70.
[9] Ibid., p. 165.

Freud's third form of masochism, what he terms 'feminine masochism', is also relevant to our discussion because

> There is an obvious similarity between the situation in altruistic surrender and the conditions which determine male homosexuality.[10]

In his discussion of feminine masochism as found in men Freud begins by noting that

> The obvious interpretation, and one easily arrived at, is that the masochist wants to be treated like a small and helpless child, but, particularly, like a naughty child. It is unnecessary to quote cases to illustrate this; for the material is very uniform and is accessible to any observer, even to non-analysts. But if one has had the opportunity of studying cases in which the masochistic phantasies have been particularly richly elaborated, one quickly discovers that they place the subject in a characteristically female situation; they signify, that is, being castrated, or copulated with, or giving birth to a baby.[11]

Here, the factor which connects moral and erotogenic masochism with their 'natural' prototype – feminine masochism – seems to be *identification*. What Freud is saying above is that the men in question want to be treated like – that is, *are identifying with* – members of the opposite sex in situations which emphasize their passiveness and proneness to masculine, aggressive assaults. What seems to be injurious to them in these instances is only injurious to their masculine, active role. Evidently other, compensating gratifications exist which mean that although masochism hurts some aspects of the masochist it rewards others so that, for instance, erotogenic masochism may be physically painful (as when it involves real punishment) but psychologically extremely gratifying (as when it enables a man to enjoy imagining that he is a woman). Again, moral masochism may mean terrible conscious psychological suffering for the moral masochist but

[10] A. Freud, *The Ego and the Mechanisms of Defence*, p. 134.
[11] S. Freud, 'The Economic Problem of Masochism', XIX, p. 162.

may bring important unconscious satisfaction in its train (for instance, by assuaging a latent sense of guilt).

If some degree of submission to active, masculine sexual advances is normal for women and if their adult sexual role involves some degree of passiveness, then it is possible to understand much apparent masochism as based on identification with this role in either sex (since, inevitably, female sexuality will never be completely 'feminine' in this respect, as Freud pointed out).

In a discussion of altruism, erotogenic and feminine masochism are not our immediate concern, but they do enable us to understand how basic instinctual drives may become mobilized through the mechanism of identification with the consequence that if some inhibition prevents a feminine identification from expressing itself in an overtly erotic form of masochism it may nevertheless do so in a *sublimated* (that is, desexualized and disguised) manner. In this way unconscious infantile phantasies which see the female sexual role as one inevitably involving maltreatment, submission to injustice and humiliation, pain and suffering, may become indirectly gratified through experiencing all these things in a more generalized and less specific way – in short, in moral masochism.

We can now begin to understand how passiveness and a tendency to welcome pain, punishment and other perverse gratifications may be the outcome, not of direct genetic programming as the cruder biological determinists might want to argue (it is certainly hard to understand what adaptive role such tendencies could fulfil), but of a more basic mechanism – identification – which is in its turn almost certainly founded on genetic factors predisposing human beings to manifest kin altruism.

Nevertheless, this insight only pushes the problem of masochism in particular and self-injuring altruism in general back one stage further: now we need to know why human beings should come to make such identifications as those which might lead – and often have led – to them voluntarily seeking out opportunities to be maltreated, tortured, abused and humiliated. For the simple fact is that an objective approach to human altruism will make no real headway until these rather bizarre instances of self-sacrifice are fully explained, because it is these instances in particular which are often taken to be the supreme examples of heroic asceticism and ultimate self-sacrifice in terms of the subjective definition of altruism. We must now turn to consider the possibility that the answer to this question may be found in the circumstances which lead to the most important and fateful identifications which human beings ever make – those arising during childhood.

Identification and the dynamic theory of socialization

In the static, holistic, 'steady-state' social theories which were dominant until a few years ago socialization was seen as an unproblematic process by means of which an all-powerful and determining 'culture', 'collective conscience', 'ideology' or 'normative consensus' was seen as moulding individuals to its demands. The individuals in question – principally the young – were seen as passive recipients of this cultural moulding and failure on their part to approximate to its demands was called 'deviancy', 'anomie' or 'alienation'. Whilst it is true that a few sociologists protested against this 'over-socialized' view of human nature,[12] few seemed to be able to offer anything better or to even begin to conceive that socialization might be a more complex, dynamic interaction.

Yet this is what psychoanalysis has always insisted: that the interaction between parents and children in childhood is *dynamic* and typified by the conflict of opposing forces. Socialization in psychoanalytic theory is seen as a far more complex, genuinely interactive phenomenon than in any sociological theory which has appeared up to now. Indeed,

[12] D. Wrong, 'The Over-socialized Conception of Man in Modern Sociology', *The American Sociological Review*, XXVI, 1961, pp. 184–93.

until Trivers' theory of parent–offspring conflict was put forward recently it was the only theory of socialization with any real claim to being dynamic in the psychological sense.

One of the most notable errors of cultural-determinist theories, albeit one so widely disseminated that it is currently accepted as self-evidently true by just about everybody, is that socialization – in other words, parent–child conflict resolved to the satisfaction of the parents – always and everywhere occurs during childhood.

Yet, contrary to the expectations of the cultural-determinist theories, there are good reasons for thinking that this is by no means always true and may indeed only have become true relatively recently in human history. Societies such as those found in Australia prior to the arrival of Europeans certainly seem to suggest otherwise and, if they can be taken to represent something of the reality of pre-agricultural hunter-gatherer societies throughout the world, argue for a very different view of the origins of socialization. When we recall that primal hunter-gatherer societies have comprised the basic social type throughout the greater part of the time spent by *Homo sapiens* on this earth, the facts relating to the original form of human socialization cannot but be significant.

In the case of such societies the principal form of socialization (at least for boys) appears to be the dramatic initiation rituals which occur during adolescence, so that during childhood little in the way of parental moulding is to be seen. As Roheim's fieldwork makes clear, there is little or no exercise of parental authority over the young in childhood, less attempt to indoctrinate or train the young and virtually no parentally-imposed instinctual renunciations regarding weaning, infantile sexual activities, or toilet-training. When missionaries at the Hermannsberg mission first tried to discipline children in the mission school with corporal punishment a near riot broke out because the adults could not understand how anyone could beat a child in cold blood for disciplinary purposes. Aboriginal children were never beaten in such circumstances and, although a child might be slapped by an adult in a fit of temper, the child's usual response was a counter-blast of verbal abuse followed by a quick escape. An indulgent regime of child-rearing certainly made the aborigines easily resort to violence, but never in the service of parental correction, which is why the missionaries' penal practices aroused such disgust and indignation among a people who were inclined to violence but not to cruelty.[13]

Although children in such societies seem to learn as much, if not more, from each other and from older children than they do from their parents (an observation which includes speech, with many such societies having distinct 'children's languages'), some minimal degree of parental moulding nevertheless exists, as one might expect. Although no real attempt to instil what analysts would call the superego occurs until puberty and initiation, Roheim does report that mothers will induce a minimal level of superego organization when, for instance, they warn children not to wander off into the bush because of the monsters lurking there. This attempt to mould by instilling fear he terms a 'phobic' level of superego development and it seems to be as far as such developments go in childhood.

Nevertheless, during initiation some sort of more organized superego is instilled by means of what can only be called more-or-less willingly accepted corporal punishment and torture, invariably culminating in some genital mutilation such as circumcision or its symbolic equivalent, such as scarification, knocking out of teeth, tearing out of finger nails and so on.

Such maltreatment, even if only more-or-less willingly accepted, reminds us of our central problem: that of altruism, identification and masochism; for it is clear that, to the extent that such trials and tortures characterize initiation ceremonies the world over – and they are not, of course, limited to the

[13] G. Roheim, *Children of the Desert*, pp. 73–6. A further example of this, along with the power of identification in primitive people, is provided by the many reports of aboriginals in Australia openly weeping when they saw the beatings administered to criminals shipped to the penal colonies there.

primitive world[14] – they are clearly instances of masochism. But they are also equally clearly instances of masochism brought about by identification because it is their overriding desire to be accepted as adult men and to transcend the status of children that drives the initiates on to accept such punishments. They put up with it because they aspire to the identity of adults, with all the privileges which this brings – not least, of course, the sexual ones. In order to achieve this coveted, privileged status they have to prove that they are worthy of it and, in so doing, inevitably make their desire to identify with their fathers the reason why they more-or-less willingly accept the punishment inflicted on them: identification – this time with the fathers – once again motivates an instance of masochism.

Altruistic foundations of the incest-taboo

In such small-scale societies as those of the Australian aborigines where small groups of kin will wander over large distances searching for food it is easy to see that most interactions of an altruistic sort might come under the heading of kin altruism, and it will come as no surprise to learn that the preferred form of marriage is one compatible with the theory of inclusive fitness. Yet, strangely, cultural prohibitions exist which the theory does not seem to predict and which look much more like instances of altruism based on religious and moral rules. Among the most notable of these are the complex prohibitions against eating certain things which come under the heading of totemic prohibitions.

These cover a wide range of ritual avoidances relating to animals that may not be killed or eaten, plants which may not

[14] Some years ago, an American student who had attended some lectures I gave on the evolution of initiation ritual wrote me a letter saying how astonished he had been to realize that such occurrences are found in entry-ordeals into some fraternities and sororities in American universities, and included a press-cutting relating to how one unfortunate student had been found nearly dead from exposure in a campus pond, having had to brave it, naked, during a winter night.

be harvested, places which may not be visited without certain ritual constraints, and so on. They are closely linked with social avoidances which relate mostly to sexual relations, and, in particular, to taboos against incest. Totemic clans are exogamous (that is, men must marry out of them) and carry a complex array of ritual prohibitions and tribal lore which comes into full force for an individual once he is initiated. Indeed, it is not too much of an exaggeration to say that the greater part of aboriginal religion can be seen as initiation ritual continued and repeated throughout life, in some instances along with the genital mutilations.[15]

Although, as we shall see in a moment, such institutions do have elements of reciprocity about them, in the main part such ritual obligations and moral prohibitions as are imposed at initiation and dramatized in its transparent ritual and mutilations are instances of kin altruism. They represent culturally-enforced renunciations of individual instinctual gratification and self-interest in the name of tradition, morality and civilization brought about by means of identification with the chief agents of tradition, morality and civilization – the tribal fathers. They are genuine elements of rudimentary socialization and they relate to that institution of the personality which analysts call the superego and, in the manner which we saw in the previous section, draw on self-directed sadistic drives and moral masochism as their unconscious basis.

Looked at from another point of view, they are instances of successfully-resolved parent–offspring conflict – by which I really mean instances of conflict which have been resolved by more-or-less successful moulding of the young initiates by their fathers, the initiators. By establishing their authority over them in the most unmistakable and sadistic way, by forcing them to accept their tribal traditions and prohibitions, by mutilating their genitals and curtailing their sexual freedoms by the imposition of the ubiquitous incest-taboos,

[15] C. Badcock, *The Psychoanalysis of Culture*, pp. 16–31.

the fathers seek to resolve definitively the ritualized father-
-son conflict of initiation to their own satisfaction. This
resolution is partly enforced on the young men, but by no
means entirely: in large part – and in the psychologically
most important part – it comes about by means of more-or-
less voluntary identification with the fathers and their values
by the sons, identifications which, as we have already seen,
almost certainly ultimately rest on a genetic predisposition
not merely for parents to identify with their offspring, but
offspring with their parents. Such identifications as these
resolve the conflict of interests between fathers and sons
which fundamentally always exists, which probably bur-
geoned into massive social trauma at the time of the first
hominid hunting bands and which to this day underlies
individual developmental history in the form of the Oedipus
complex.

Yet, for all this, elements of reciprocal altruism are not
missing in primal societies. As we might expect from the
importance given to reciprocal interactions in Trivers' original theory, we find clear evidence that, alongside kin-
altruism-through-identification, there is strong evidence of
reciprocal altruism as well.

Commenting on the parallel existence of marriage classes
and totemic clans, each of which is exogamous and both of
which seem to regulate marriage, Freud says that

> The historical relation between the marriage-classes (of which
> in some tribes there are as many as eight) and the totem clans
> is completely obscure. It is merely evident that these arrange-
> ments are directed towards the same aim as totemic exogamy
> and pursue it still further. While, however, totemic exogamy
> gives one the impression of being a sacred ordinance of
> unknown origin – in short, of being a custom – the compli-
> cated institution of marriage-classes, with their subdivisions
> and regulations attaching to them, look more like the result of
> deliberate legislation, which may perhaps have taken up the
> task afresh of preventing incest because the influence of the
> totem was waning. And, while the totemic system is, as we

know, the basis of all other social obligations and moral restrictions of the tribe, the significance of the phratries seems in general not to extend beyond the regulation of marriage choice which is its aim.[16]

No doubt Freud is correct in attributing to the marriage-class system the function of bolstering and reinforcing the primary, totemic incest-prohibitions which seem so important to primal hunter-gatherers:

> The incest taboo between brother and sister is one of the most, if not *the* most stringent sexual taboos among the Australian Aborigines. Aborigines often accuse other tribes of marrying their own sisters, for nothing could be more animal-like than that.[17]

Nevertheless, I am tempted to try to throw some light on the puzzlement which Freud rightly stresses regarding the relation between these two very similar institutions and to suggest that, besides exhibiting that element of redundancy so often seen in obsessive defence-mechanisms, the marriage-class system chiefly fulfils the demands of reciprocal rather than kin altruism.

Lévi-Strauss, in his widely influential neo-Freudian analysis[18] of Australian and other prescriptive marriage-class systems, strongly inclines to the view that such systems are based fundamentally on the principle of reciprocity in the exchange of sisters.[19] Looked at from this standpoint it is tempting to see the marriage-class system of the Australian aborigines as duplicating the system of totemic exogamy but stressing not kin altruism, but reciprocal altruism. If this is the case then we can see that, in the primal hunter-gatherer cultures which we are considering, kin altruism, at least in so far as it applies to sexual prohibitions, seems to require the support of reciprocal arrangements as well, almost as if

---

[16] S. Freud, *Totem and Taboo*, XIV, 9.
[17] D. McKnight, *Australian Aborigine Marriage-class Systems* (in press).
[18] C. Badcock, *Levi-Strauss*, chapter 5, 'A footnote to Freud'.
[19] C. Lévi-Strauss, *The Elementary Structures of Kinship*.

primal hunter-gatherers were saying 'If we have to give up our sisters, we will only do so if you give up yours.' The two parallel forms of altruism, kin and reciprocal, perhaps give rise to parallel regulating institutions, both of which stress the moral obligation of avoiding incest and both of which logically imply reciprocity of sisters (since if I cannot marry my sister and you cannot marry yours, there is nothing to stop us marrying each other's); but whereas one – the totemic system – stresses the moral obligation not to commit incest, the other – the marriage-class system – stresses the obligation to exchange sisters. Both come together graphically in the common circumstance that it is a young man's circumcisor who will be expected to provide him with a bride when he is ready to marry so that aborigines customarily see the wife as the compensation for the cut.[20]

In summary then, we can say that such cultures as these exhibit minimal childhood socialization, limited to what Roheim called the phobic level of superego development; because of this they require elaborate rituals of initiation at puberty which in effect are continued throughout life as the nucleus of adult religion; finally, these rituals are instances of kin-altruism-through-identification and turn on two chief moral obligations: those relating to totemism and to exogamy, the latter being powerfully bolstered by an elaborate system of rules and regulations aimed at ensuring reciprocity in the consequences of incest-avoidance – the exchange of sisters.

Parent–child conflict in delayed-return subsistence systems

If we accept the by-no-means unreasonable proposition that the aboriginal culture of Australia represents in all probability a close approximation to that of the primal human hunter-

[20] And evidently complain bitterly if they have been 'cut for nothing'. Personal communication from Dr David McKnight.

gatherers, then we begin to glimpse a surprising realization: childhood socialization, at least on any extensive scale, may be a relatively modern innovation and may not predate the Neolithic Revolution by any great extent. Furthermore, it is also possible that, if children seem to be relatively unconstrained by their parents in primal hunter-gatherer societies, then parents may be much more constrained by their children as a consequence. This possibility is readily suggested by a theory which sees parent–child interactions as *dynamic*, that is, as based on conflict and motivated by the differing interests of the parties concerned. It really boils down to a very simple proposition: if parent–child conflict can result in success for the parents, then there is no reason why they should not also sometimes produce a win for the children.

Following on my discussion of initiation it may seem difficult to see how this can be so; after all, the fathers seem to have the upper hand: they decide when initiation is appropriate and they carry it out; furthermore, in the society as a whole they are definitely the dominant force. But the exact opposite is true of the mothers. If we restrict our attention to what turns out to be the most important instance, the parent–child conflict which we call weaning, then it seems that in primal hunter-gatherer societies the children win hands down; for, as I mentioned earlier, maternally-enforced early weaning does not seem to occur. Children are suckled on demand throughout early childhood (something which has desirable contraceptive consequences for societies constantly threatened by too many mouths to feed) and, although older children will begin to eat an adult diet, they will still be seen to have recourse to the breast on occasions at any time up to adolescence (although at these later ages for emotional, rather than dietary, sustenance). In practice, parentally-enforced weaning only occurs for boys at initiation since, although no adult man would be seen sucking at his mother's breast, any child might, and boys remain children until they become men through initiation. We might sum up by saying that, although voluntary weaning to an adult diet does occur

during childhood, enforced weaning from emotional dependency on the mother does not take place until adolescence,
which for boys means initiation.[21]

It seems that parents do not enforce any real sexual avoidances or taboos during childhood in most Australian aboriginal societies and that children exploit Oedipal ploys right up
to adolescence and only then – especially if they are boys –
feel the full force of the incest-taboo through the punishments, genital and other mutilations and moral exhortations
of initiation. Indeed, Roheim reports that Aranda parents
will not only tolerate all kinds of sexual precocity in their
children and even regard it as harmless and amusing, but that
mothers habitually sleep lying protectively on their sons
(although never their daughters).[22]

Significantly, the one operative taboo where children are
concerned – that they should not witness parental intercourse
– was largely unenforceable among a people who habitually
slept naked in the open around camp fires.[23] Such toleration
of anything short of direct observation of parental sexual
activity suggests that, at least among the central Australian
aborigines, mothers capitulated more or less completely to
the children and fathers held their hand until their progeny
were children no longer.

It seems, then, that women in primal hunter-gatherer
societies do not try very hard to counter Oedipal ploys in
general and do not enforce weaning in particular. Certainly,
ethnographic evidence suggests that they are habitually
exploited quite shamelessly by both their children (to whose
care they devote most of their free time) and their menfolk.

[21] Even in those rare instances where a definite pre-initiation weaning
ceremony occurs among Australian aborigines (as among the Lardil) it is
notably late by the standards of agricultural societies (i.e., does not occur
usually prior to age 6, and is often later). I am indebted for this information
to my colleague, Dr David McKnight.

[22] G. Roheim, *The Riddle of the Sphinx*, p. 165; 'Psychoanalysis of
Primitive Cultural Types', *International Journal of Psychoanalysis*, 23, 1932,
pp. 54 and 87: 'Nobody objects to the onanism of children and I have often
observed Tankai playing with the penis of her son, Aldinga.'

[23] Roheim, *The Riddle of the Sphinx*, p. 30.

Speaking of the Aranda, Roheim says, 'The whole culture is built on the repression of women.'[24] Such societies are notably male-dominated and although the outcome of the father–son conflict which underlies initiation is undoubtedly mainly a win for the fathers, their values and institutions, the mother–child conflict which underlies weaning seems largely to turn out to serve the interests of the child, at least in the relatively crude and obvious sense that aboriginal mothers, evidently, do not manage to wean their children until the children have weaned themselves. This observation prompts me to suggest a possible explanation for the origins of the next crucial development in human cultural evolution – namely, agriculture.

Until recently, the dominant cultural-determinist orthodoxy not only completely failed to account for cultural origins but even tried to make a virtue of its explanatory impotence and castigated any alternative theory which tried to do so. But unless we are content with the circular reasoning which insists that culture determines culture we might be better advised to look elsewhere for an explanation and could do worse than begin with the evident differences between socialization in primal hunter-gatherer societies and simple agricultural ones.

Primitive agricultural societies show marked contrasts in socialization when compared with hunter-gatherer cultures. Here weaning occurs, often traumatically, along with considerable discipline in childhood. Initiation declines in importance or even disappears altogether, but the greater importance of discipline in childhood, particularly regarding weaning and infantile sexual practices, means that the superego is normally much more developed than we find in the hunter-gatherer case (along with the propensity to sado-masochistic sexual perversions).[25]

Such societies are typified by economies based on *delayed return*, rather than the *immediate return* of primal hunter-

[24] Ibid., p. 165.
[25] Roheim, *The Riddle of the Sphinx*, p. 276.

gatherers.[26] By contrast to the hunter-gatherer way of life which is literally a 'hand-to-mouth' affair, agriculture demands an inevitable delay between planting, for instance, and harvesting (even then, something must be held back or the agriculturalist will have nothing to plant next year). This self-imposed abstinence in consumption – something which does not come at all easily to hunter-gatherers like the Australian aborigines, indeed, something which is not adaptive for their way of life – is clearly of vital importance to the success of agriculture. It is also in all probability the occasion for a profound frustration, particularly of the agriculturalist's oral-maternal attachments, because, no sooner do delayed-return systems of subsistence appear than a whole host of mother-goddesses and other anthropomorphic deities enter onto the stage of religious history, strongly suggesting that they provided a fantasied gratification in heaven for frustrations recently encountered on earth.[27]

Since we know that an ability to postpone oral instinctual gratifications – i.e., those relevant to agriculture – is reliant on successfully being weaned in childhood, it seems that here we have another form of economic life based on an instance of parent–child conflict. Indeed, weaning, even in animal populations, is an obvious case where the interests of the mother and those of the young may come into conflict. Here the conflict is not some primeval war between foraging fathers and their hunter sons, but a more private, intimate one between mother and child which is almost inevitable but, in the context of agriculture, becomes of vital significance. In primal hunter-gatherer societies it seems that the adaptive necessities of the immediate-return mode of subsistence work on the side of the child in making weaning undesirable, and the resulting unweaned, unworried-about-subsistence, character-type highly suitable to their variable and unreliable food resources. In an economy where hunger or even actual

[26] J. Woodburn, 'Hunters and Gatherers Today and Reconstruction of the Past', in E. Gellner (ed.), *Soviet and Western Anthropology*.
[27] For a fuller account see Badcock, *Madness and Modernity*, chapter 2.

starvation can threaten at any time and where the crucial resource – game – is largely outside the control of the hunters, weaning-induced anxiety about the future of food supplies is clearly not adaptive.

In agriculture, however, such anxieties are vital and most of the economic advantages appear to fall on the side of the mother who, we presume, has an interest in rather earlier weaning than the child might wish. Indeed, the dynamics of the origins of agriculture may well be found in the reactions of what were perhaps the more masculine women in primal hunter-gatherer economies who reacted against an excessively feminine, maternal role which denied them any real scope for the expression of other aspects of their personalities. In primal societies men are the hunters, women the gatherers, so it is not unlikely that women were the first to experiment with the domestication of plants. In the light of the present discussion we can also envisage the possibility that the change to agriculture was an outcome, in part at least, both of a weaning-conflict between mothers and children, and of a more general sexual conflict between men and women.

Where climatic and other factors became favourable it may have been the case that at least some women in male-dominated hunter-gatherer societies should have realized an opportunity to assert the more active side of their personalities, not merely in becoming actively involved with planting rather than just harvesting what nature provided, but in weaning their children and playing a more dominant role in socialization. The beginnings of agriculture may have provided an opportunity for women to assert themselves both in mother–child relations and in more general male–female ones, with women turning their previously largely passive gathering activities into a vital new resource. Armed with a newly relevant expertise and poised to exploit the many opportunities offered by a shift to a novel mode of subsistence, women could not only have begun to win the weaning conflict with their children but also win a previously unprecedented and much more prominent role for themselves in society and culture as a whole.[28]

As far as children were concerned, the coming of weaning in early childhood reversed a trend probably not interrupted since an early point in human evolution. As I argued earlier, neoteny could well have been the anatomical, evolutionary expression of a regressive ploy in parent–offspring interactions. Its practical effect was to make human infants much more passively dependent on the parents – and on the mother in particular – than most other mammals, and for a much longer period of time. During the first year or two of childhood the human neonate is wholly dependent on the parents for feeding, protection and transportation over any significant distance (the latter being an important matter in primal, nomadic societies). Since all its early feeding needs must originally have been provided by the breasts of the mother it is not surprising that Freud termed the first period of psychosexual development the 'oral phase' or that he found important latent attachments to oral factors remaining in the unconscious throughout life. Indeed, it is possible that a unique human anatomical feature of such dependency is represented by the evolution of lips, which may have evolved to give more obvious expression to the oral requirements of the child and which also play a prominent role in the facial expressiveness of adults – not to mention sexual behaviours such as kissing.

It seems that weaning ended the long-standing success of the human child in its campaign to exploit its mother for maximum investment in itself and heralded an epoch-marking change in which parental interests began to become more dominant. It also probably marks the beginning of a shift in the time at which enforced identifications of children with their parents occurred, moving back from the period of

[28] For a fuller discussion of this point see Badcock, *The Psychoanalysis of Culture*, pp. 87–93, and *Madness and Modernity*, chapter 2.

adolescence and initiation to that of early childhood and weaning. Now, instead of being brought about by the ordeals of entry into adult life, identification with the parent came about through denial of the breast. Psychoanalytic investigations of object-loss – and weaning is primarily an object-loss – suggest that the typical response is identification with, and introjection of, the lost object. The thing which can no longer actually be incorporated by sucking – the breast, and the mother to which it is attached – now becomes psychologically incorporated by identification. In a memorable phrase of Freud's, 'the shadow of the object falls across the ego' and identification with the parent comes about through the new ordeal of weaning.[29]

Such a fundamental and early identification with the parent partly fulfils the role of the adolescent identifications brought about through initiation which we discussed above. In more advanced cultures, those which have evolved to the pastoral or industrial stage, there are reasons for supposing that further instinctual renunciations are enforced by parents during infancy. For instance, it seems that toilet-training becomes especially prominent because of its known relationship with aggressive drives and because the reaction-formations to which it gives rise – thrift, orderliness and obstinacy – are especially useful in economies like pastoral or industrial ones where capital needs to be accumulated and where the greatest economic returns usually follow from the greatest investments, be they of money, time or effort.[30]

Anyone who has ever tried to toilet-train a child will not need to be told that it is an instance of parent–offspring conflict, and an unmistakable one at that. Excremental attitudes and behaviour of primal hunter-gatherers leave little doubt that they do not share the inhibitions of peoples who

[29] See S. Freud's classic paper, 'Mourning and Melancholia', XIV, 243-58.
[30] For a fuller discussion of this point see C. Badcock, *The Psychoanalysis of Culture*, chapters 3 and 4.

belong to societies at higher levels of economic development,[31] and it does not take much insight to see that toilet-training, no matter how sensitively carried out by the parents, is always ultimately an attempt to coerce the child into conformity with culturally-approved attitudes and behaviour regarding its excremental activities.

As in the comparable case of submission to parental coercion during initiation, toilet-training and the even more important submission to counter-Oedipal incest-taboos during childhood result in typical identifications with the parents and their values. Just as the aboriginal initiate is forced to undergo various contrived ordeals in order to prove his worthiness to be admitted to adult male society and has implicitly thereby to prove the reliability of his identification with the tribal fathers, so the child in higher cultures has to endure the ordeals of weaning and toilet-training in order to win parental approval and in a comparable way attest identification with the parents and their values. It is almost as if the child, realizing that it was on the losing side in the weaning/toilet-training/Oedipal conflicts adopted the if-you-can't-beat-them-join-them tactic and capitulated to the parents by means of a particularly primitive and effective type of identification which, in so far as the parents can be seen as playing the dominant, aggressive role, is called 'identification with the aggressor'.

This is in part at least a continuation in human psychology of a common behavioural trait of most primates in which attacks on one member of a dominance hierarchy by an individual above it result in the attacked animal turning on one beneath it rather than its original and superior antagonist.

[31] An amusing and typical example of this was provided recently by a colleague (Dr David McKnight) who informed me that newcomers to an aboriginal settlement which he knew hit on the expedient of covering themselves with their excrement in order to keep other occupants at a distance! A greater contrast with the fastidiousness of primitive pastoralists, who will often not so much as mention excrement, can hardly be imagined.

In a similar way children will very often deal with an assault on them like the Jewish children playing at Nazi storm-troopers mentioned earlier. In a manner inexplicable to cultural-determinist theories of socialization, children will often respond to an attack by identifying with the aggressor in such a way that they redirect their own aggression in a manner which makes them seem to be not so much the targets of the attack, but its instigators. When such behaviour occurs in the context of oral, anal and phallic developmental crises in childhood we have the fundamental behavioural foundations for the identifications with the parents and their cultural values which psychoanalysis calls the superego, and which any genuinely dynamic theory of parent–child interaction will also find as the psychological foundation of all delayed-return cultures which rely on internalized restraint by psychological agencies rather than external coercion by agencies of social control.

Identification and generalized kin altruism

There seems to be one respect in which both cultural-determinism and the cruder forms of biological determinism resemble one another: this is their tendency not to do justice to the full complexity of human behaviour and to the full perversity of human psychology. Both, in their different ways, oversimplify and caricature the reality of human beings by ignoring the fact that between both cultural and genetic determinants of behaviour there is a psychological mechanism which, for sheer elaboration and complexity, probably has few rivals in the entirety of creation. Furthermore, the dynamic nature of this psychological mechanism means that few things which affect it can have simple or direct results because it interacts with, and feeds back to, both the stimulus in many cases and very often also to its own reaction to it. When we add to this the fact that its reactions will often be ambivalent, multifaceted and contradictory, we come up with a mechanism which is wonderful indeed in both the degree and the extent of its complications.

Neither biologists, ethologists, nor even primatologists encounter quite such complex psychological behaviour in the subjects of their disciplines. To the extent that sociology and the other social sciences have concerned themselves more or less exclusively with the abstractions of holistic social theory – 'social structure', 'dialectics', 'collective consciousness', etc. – nor do they, because these abstractions, although often complex in themselves, are simple and straightforward when compared with the elaborate subtleties of human psychology. It seems that only psychoanalysis has concerned itself with the human mind in all its glorious and often perverse involution. Yet this preoccupation, while at the root of much of the resistance to this latest advance in scientific insight, is also the reason why psychoanalysis is in an especially favourable position to be able to remedy the very evident shortcomings of the cruder cultural and biological determinisms.

The whole question of the generalization of kin altruism is a case in point. Are we seriously to believe that every particular behaviour which demonstrates kin altruism among human beings has its own specific genetic determinants comparable to those specific genetic determinants which, for instance, almost certainly underlie the behaviour of soldiers in insect societies? Do human soldiers have genes for patriotic self-sacrifice? I very much doubt it. Again, are we seriously expected to believe, in the face of all the difficulties attending on cultural-determinism, that human beings are somehow exempted from the laws of biology and free to bestow their altruistic attentions indiscriminately? Although many would like to have us believe that they would (or, it would be more accurate to say, that they *should*), Darwinian and Freudian insights into altruism can explain this tendency to advocate indiscriminate altruism as not so much an exception to biological principles, but a product of them. The fact that nature abhors altruism need not be taken to mean that biology cannot explain why culture adores it. Psychoanalysis, however, provides the basis for a sound theory linking specific genetic determinants of kin altruism – the hypothesized and empirically well-founded tendency to form identifications – with the full range and elaboration of actual human behaviour.

At first sight the idea of generalized kin altruism may seem contradictory, and so, I suppose, it would be in the case of most other species. But in our own the situation is different because, as we have already seen, behaviours which promote kin altruism are not normally to be expected to be under tight genetic control. If we contrast two very comparable circumstances, soldiers in insect societies and in human ones, we immediately see that, compared to the human case, insect soldier behaviour is much less problematic and much more simply related to genetic controls. Unlike human warriors, soldier ants or termites are not subject to ambivalence, conflicts of conscience or the temptation to run away, desert to the enemy or otherwise to behave in inappropriate ways. All these complications arise out of the complex interactive nature of human psychology which, I would argue, serves to provide the dynamic interface between genes and behaviour.

In the case of self-sacrifice on the battlefield, human soldiers, like insect ones, are often acting in accordance with kin altruism, but, in the human case, this kin altruism comes about via the dynamic psychological link of identification. In primal hunter-gatherer societies – where, significantly, warfare as such is unknown – what passes for conflict on the large scale takes place in desultory skirmishes between local groups whose members, as likely as not, tend to be kin. In more advanced societies, where full-scale warfare can and does exist, identification with some symbolic kin-group such as the tribe, nation or regiment takes the place of primal kin-identifications. Indeed, military psychology stresses the need for 'morale' – that is, positive group-identification – in the success of military action of all kinds, not to mention loyalty to – another manifestation of *identification with* – the country, king, commander, or whatever.

Of course, such kin-altruism-through-identification is not the whole story. The complexities of human dynamic psychology mean that pure forms of motivation are seldom found. In the case of our soldiers, for instance, we can readily see that the situation may be different. If the soldiers in question have been drafted into service by the threat of sanctions against them we are clearly dealing, not with altruism-through-identification, but with altruism brought about by coercion. To the extent that most soldiers are paid (and especially so in the case of mercenaries), they receive a personal reciprocal benefit for their services – an obvious instance of reciprocal altruism. Nevertheless, to the extent that human soldiers may be seen as acting in accordance with the principles of kin altruism, it is by no means unreasonable to suggest that, rather than being directly motivated to do so by genes for patriotism or military self-sacrifice, their behaviour comes about, in part at least, through the mechanism of identification with individuals, social groups, values, or institutions which are psychologically appropriate.

Another example of the utility of the theory of kin-altruism-through-identification might be taken from deterministic excesses from the other, cultural side. The existence of the social institution of the avunculate – the prominence given to the mother's brother in many primitive societies – has been taken by many anthropologists and sociologists as evidence of the efficacy of cultural determinism. It is usually assumed that, whereas biology might have something to say about the so-called 'nuclear family' of father, mother and children, it had to concede defeat to cultural determinism in explaining the social significance of the mother's brother, an allegedly social rather than biologically-defined role.

But consider the following alternative interpretation. There is no denying that, in all societies, maternity is always much more certain than paternity. In societies where there is a significant degree of pre-marital and extra-marital sexual activity a man's confidence that his children are really his own is bound to be weakened. This is very often the case in matrilineal societies, by contrast to patrilineal ones, because in the latter emphasis on virginity at marriage and proscription of adultery is often very marked. Consequently, the more fluid and unpredictable sexual situation in matrilineal societies may incline them to the avunculate because

> *a general society-wide lowering of confidence of paternity will lead to a society-wide prominence, or institutionalization, of mother's brother as an appropriate male dispenser of parental benefits.* We can add that to the extent that paternal care is more appropriately directed to males, mother's brother may be expected to attend more to sister's sons than to sister's daughters.[32]

In short, far from vindicating cultural determinism, the institution of the avunculate may be in large part a consequence of the basic theorems of kin altruism and parental investment: it may simply be the case that, in societies where paternity is doubtful, it would pay a man's genes if he were to invest more in his sister's children than his own because his genetic relatedness to them is relatively much more certain.

But how is this behaviour to come about? Are we to assume that mother's brothers are conscious of both the theory of kin altruism and parental investment? Or are we to suppose that there are genes for avuncular behaviour present in matrilineal cultures but lacking in patrilineal ones? Obviously, both alternatives are absurd; but that need not necessarily mean that we must content ourselves with unenlightening cultural-determinist explanations which depict some cultural conventions as caused by other cultural conventions.

On the contrary, it is certainly possible, and far from absurd, to argue that the behaviour in question in fact comes about because of the mechanism of identification of fathers

[32] R. D. Alexander, *Darwinism and Human Affairs*, p. 172. Author's emphasis.

with children. In patrilineal societies the numerous safe-
guards against confusions in paternity reinforce a man's
natural tendency to identify with, and therefore to act altruistically towards, his own children; but in matrilineal ones
where sexual relations are more fluid and unpredictable a
man's natural tendency to identify with his own children
might be weakened by uncertainties about whether they
were his. He might consequently compensate by identifying
more with those of his sister with whom, in a matrilineal
culture, he is in any case likely to identify rather more
strongly than in a patrilineal one (because both belong to the
same matrilineal kin group).

In this circumstance, once again, the dynamic psychological mechanism of identification will have fulfilled the
demands of kin altruism in a typical way. It is not that genes
for such altruism do not exist, as the cultural-determinists
argue, or that they are all that exists, as the cruder biological
determinists want to claim, but that the only genes likely to
be able to motivate kin altruism in human beings are those
which presumably underlie the innate psychological tendency to form dynamic identifications.

Freud's declaration that 'Identification is known to psychoanalysis as the earliest expression of an emotional tie with
another person'[33] points towards the considerable psychological evidence underpinning the contention that identification is basic to kin altruism in human beings.[34] The element
of altruism comes about, evidently, by making individuals
identify with others to the extent of doing for them what
they might otherwise only do for themselves. Yet one of

[33] S. Freud, *Group Psychology and the Analysis of the Ego*, XVIII, 105.

[34] A delightful example of the fundamental nature of identification and
its relation with altruism was provided by one of my sons at about the age
of eighteen months. Seeing me one day deep in thought and absent-
mindedly sucking a finger nail, he toddled off to his bedroom, returned
with his dummy (to which at the time he was much addicted) and thrust it
into my mouth. It seems that even a toddler can identify with another
person to the extent of correctly intuiting an oral need in them and can
perform an act of significant altruism in offering a possession of his own to
satisfy it.

Freud's most important insights was that this ability to over-come one's sense of difference from – and indifference to – the other is a consequence, not of an innate tendency to form indiscriminate identifications with other people, but of the dynamic structure of the process of identification itself.

As we have already seen, the earliest and most fundamental identifications come about during early childhood and are a part of the dynamic interactions between parental figures and children. What Freud discovered in his work on mass, as opposed to individual, psychology was that the kinds of identifications on which large groups depend come about as a consequence of those much earlier and more intimate identi-fications within the family circle. He demonstrated in his classic work, *Group Psychology and the Analysis of the Ego*, that individuals in groups do not achieve identification with one another by a direct, conscious and simple means, even if the size of the group made this a practical proposition, which it often does not. On the contrary, his investigations showed that identification within the group comes about by a subtle, unconscious and indirect means, one which takes the proto-typical identifications of childhood for their model and builds upon them in a characteristic way.

His central finding was that the individual's ego does not identify with the individual egos of all other members of the social group in question, but that identification comes about because the individuals in the group have each formed a common identification with someone, or something else, which thereby acts as a focus for the group. Yet, in order to submit to the greater or lesser loss of individual autonomy which membership of any psychological group demands, he found that the individual's ego would only accept an identifi-cation with something which it regarded as suitable. His insights into ego-psychology showed him that the indi-vidual's ego was most likely to accept as a candidate for its identifications something modelled on prototypes of identifi-cation from childhood. In other words, he found that the ego needed entities with which to identify which resembled those to which it had already formed satisfactory identifications in the past. These past identifications of the ego were internalized in what he termed the *superego*, or *ego ideal* – that part of the ego differentiated by being based on identification with, and internalization of, parental figures. Consequently, his finding was that '*A primary group of this kind is a number of individuals who have put one and the same object in the place of their ego ideal and have consequently identified themselves with one another in their ego.*'[35]

This insight explains why all psychological groups – that is, those formed by the psychological process of identification – need either a leader, an object or an ideal with which their members' egos can form identifications after the model of those which they formed with parental figures in childhood. Since such identifications are dynamically dependent on the childhood ones, and since the latter were almost certainly programmed by evolution for purposes of what we are calling kin altruism – that is, altruism based on parents' genetic relatedness to their children and their children's genetic relatedness to them – it must now be clear how, thanks to the psychological mechanisms involved, basic kin altruism can become generalized to social groupings much larger than the immediate family, indeed to social groupings which embrace the local community, tribe, nation or race.

Although such groupings may seem far away from their psychological prototypes, their basic structure and many of their incidental characteristics are conditioned by it. However much group leaders may preach 'pure' altruism and selfless commitment to the interests of the group, their tendency to style themselves *fathers* of the nation, servants of the *mother*land, or leaders of their *brothers* or *sisters*, transparently reveals the latent kin altruism which such groupings try to exploit. Indeed, it seems that all societies which organize themselves on the basis of traditional, inherited authority or on ethnic, national or other allegedly genetic foundations are

---

[35] S. Freud, *Group Psychology and the Analysis of the Ego*, XVIII, 116. Freud's emphasis.

exploiting this tendency to extend, generalize and exploit the dynamic psychological mechanisms which motivate basic kin altruism in human beings. If we are justified in speaking of an 'expanding circle'[36] of human altruism then the mechanism of identification is one of the principal means by which this expansion comes about.

Unless this approach to the problem is fundamentally flawed, it becomes unmistakably clear that biological theories regarding kin altruism cannot be reliably applied to human beings unless their dynamic psychological consequences are fully appreciated. Furthermore, this example, like all the preceding ones in this book, suggests that the dynamic psychological processes in question are, in large part at least, already well known and that Freud seems in this context a natural successor to Darwin, and psychoanalysis a necessary adjunct to sociobiology, at least in so far as it is applied to human beings.

Compulsion and consciousness

This discussion of identification and kin altruism suggests the following question: why, if identification serves the interests of kin altruism, should it remain *unconscious*? It would seem that the sociobiological theory of the evolution of the unconscious could hardly apply here since, in the first place, we are talking, not of reciprocal altruism, but of kin altruism; and, secondly, there seems no need to practise a deceit on oneself if one is genuinely acting altruistically, albeit by means of identification. Why, if one puts oneself in someone else's place by identifying with them, should one wish to remain unaware of the fact? Surely here, if nowhere else, one would want one's altruistic identification to be apparent.

The answer to this question is that to a limited extent one may indeed tend to become conscious of such creditable identifications, but analysis shows that a part always tends to

[36] I refer to the book of this title by P. Singer.

remain unconscious, and very often the entire process of identification remains unconscious too. A paradigmatic example might be provided by the system of dynamic identifications which underlies what we might term 'punitive monotheism' among nomadic pastoralists.

In their enthusiasm for their own achievements, human beings often forget that such characteristically cultural adaptations as agriculture and pastoralism have distinct natural equivalents among the social insects, where species of ant practise both a form of agriculture (the raising of crops of fungi) and a form of pastoralism (by means of which aphids and other insects are exploited for their sugary secretions). In both cases it would not be at all far-fetched to suggest that the adaptations in question were fairly directly under genetic and chemical control. Yet, for reasons which were discussed above, it is most unlikely that the same rather simple kinds of explanation would work for human pastoralists or agriculturalists. Even though genes for the production of the milk-digesting enzyme *lactase* might be preferentially distributed among pastoralists and agriculturalists who rely on milk as a part of the diet,[37] I would be very much surprised if anyone ever isolated genes for pastoralism or agriculture as such. On the contrary, comparative sociological studies of societies in which both migratory pastoral and settled agricultural adaptations are found suggest that the differences most relevant are not genetic as such, but psychological.[38]

Analysis of the cases of pastoralists like the Nuer and Dinka of the Sudan shows that, as our general theory would lead us to expect, the equivalent determining mechanism to the kin altruism which underlies insect agriculture and pastoralism is dynamic identification. Anthropologists report that between the pastoralist and his beasts there exists a notable and unmistakable identification, by means of which

[37] N. Kretchmer, 'Lactose and Lactase', *Scientific American*, 227, 1972, pp. 70-8.
[38] R. B. Edgerton, *The Individual in Cultural Adaptation*. See also Badcock, *The Psychoanalysis of Culture*, chapter 3.

men identify both themselves and members of their families with the cattle.[39]

However, this identification is largely unconscious and, indeed, *compulsive*, as the following instance illustrates. In the case of the Dinka, ritual specialists exist called 'Masters of the Fishing Spear' whose clan-totem is Flesh. The fascinating associations – reported by anthropologists, be it noted, who could not be accused of any Freudian proclivities – between blood, incest and parricide which Dinka Flesh totemism reveals cannot detain us here,[40] but what is worthy of notice is the fact that identification with Flesh is apparently quite involuntary. This is revealed by the case of a Christian informant of the anthropologist who confessed to him that he dared not attend animal sacrifices for fear of being seized by a fit of uncontrollable trembling caused, according to Dinka lore, through possession by the spirit of his totem. Evidently this made the Christian Dinka's own flesh imitate the twitching seen in the flesh of newly-slaughtered animals and can have no other psychological explanation than that it was brought about by a dynamic and indeed compulsive identification.[41]

Furthermore, the psycho-dynamics of the entire culture and the explanation of the often-noted correspondence between primitive pastoralism and what we could call 'punitive monotheism' is based ultimately on a mechanism of dynamic identification by means of which cattle – the prime economic resource of pastoral peoples – are unconsciously and compulsively identified with the parents. As far as the positive, loving side of the pastoralist's feelings towards his own kin is concerned, there is no problem. Rather like people in other cultures who will, for instance, adopt pets and treat them as members of the family (often as surrogate children), 'cattle-breeding tribes are cattle-loving tribes.'[42]

[39] E. Evans-Pritchard, *Nuer Religion*, p. 249.
[40] See Badcock, *The Psychoanalysis of Culture*, pp. 106–8.
[41] Ibid., p. 107; G. Lienhardt, *Divinity and Experience*, p. 138.
[42] G. Roheim, *The Origin and Function of Culture*, p. 65; and Badcock, *The Psychoanalysis of Culture*, p. 109.

Yet positive, loving feelings are not the only ones engendered by close kin. We saw earlier that, thanks to the inevitability of parent–offspring conflict, ambivalence is to be expected and, as the transparently Oedipal Flesh folklore of the Dinka suggests, there are considerable negative, hating feelings also involved. But how are these to be disposed of? Clearly, pastoral peoples rely on their herds for food, yet they do not normally slaughter to satisfy hunger. In fact, the major source of protein is usually not meat, but milk and blood (the latter bled off the animals, usually at the jugular vein). Among exquisite pastoral nomads like the Nuer and Dinka animals may only be killed for religious sacrifice. Nothing is more reprehensible in their eyes than to slaughter to assuage hunger – only religious duty can excuse it, an obvious adaptation as far as the conservation of the herds is concerned.

It is here that negative, sadistic drives which might be directed towards the herds cause a problem because the temptation engendered by being surrounded by hundreds or thousands of tame, defenceless beasts must be considerable, especially if one is hungry. Such dangerous, sadistic drives are dealt with by a typical unconscious defence-mechanism: they are *projected*, and in being disposed of in this way provide an explanation for the other notable cultural adaptation of such peoples – their tendency to manifest a punitive form of monotheism.

The Dinka and Nuer are typified, from the religious point of view, by being monotheists whose God lives in the sky, and who controls the crucial resource for nomadic pastoralists – the rain. He has no anthropomorphic form even though he is addressed as 'Father of Men',[43] and his chief function seems to be to punish sin. This is why I described this form of monotheism as 'punitive', and comparative psychological studies of pastoralists show them to be more

[43] Evans-Pritchard, *Nuer Religion*, p. 7.

than usually prone to feelings of guilt and mild depression.[44] Certainly, accounts of the Nuer and the Dinka show them to be remarkably ready to accept ill-fortune as the just chastisements of God and characteristically given to fastidious examination of conscience.

The explanation of both these characteristics – the punitive form of monotheism and the personality-structure of the pastoralists – is to be found in the fact that the negative, sadistic side of the ambivalence mobilized by identification of the cattle with the parents is projected onto the deity, who now symbolically wields against the pastoralist the very same aggressive drives which he cannot afford to allow himself to turn against the herds on which he depends. In such a punitive monotheism individuals are punishing themselves for their unconscious sadism with that very same sadism: they repress it in themselves by projective means – it is denied access to consciousness but re-inflicted on the self by the phantasied agency of the deity. This deity functions both as the projected focus for group-identification (making the larger kin group into a psychological group), and also as a channel for aggression which, because it cannot be allowed to threaten the herds, is turned back against those unworthy enough to feel it in the first place.

In turning back an aggressive drive in this way the deity functions as an ego ideal and is, indeed, modelled in a fairly obvious way on the individual's own superego. By stressing fairly fastidious and punitive toilet-training – the infantile instance of parent–offspring conflict relating to sadistic drives and ultimately involving coercion of the child's excremental activities into what is expected by the parents – a superego is constituted in childhood which forms the basis for the wider, religious group-identifications of adult life. Aggressive drives mastered by the individual superego in childhood are placed at the disposal of the cultural superego during adult life and thereby constitute the psychological foundation both of religion and the pastoral adaptation.

[44] Badcock, *The Psychoanalysis of Culture*, pp. 116–21; Edgerton, *The Individual*.

If we now return to our original question after this lengthy but significant digression into the further ramifications of dynamic identification and human kin altruism, we can now perhaps begin to discern an answer. If we ask ourselves specifically why, in the case of punitive monotheists like the Nuer and Dinka, the greater part of the psychological process of identification needs to remain unconscious we can immediately see that *it is because it is unconscious that it remains compulsive,* and that it must be compulsive in this instance if it is to be effective. This is because if the whole conflict were to become conscious it would no longer be based on a compulsive projective mechanism but on rational insight. What had been imagined to exist objectively outside of consciousness – the recriminating God of the punitive monotheist – would now be recognized as existing within him as an identification within his ego. Since the ego is the executive agency of the personality it is capable of some degree of adaptation to reality, as well as to its instinctual drives. In this instance it discovers that what it thought was a part of external reality is in fact a derivative of itself; but it also sees that this part of itself is a reality, albeit an internal one, and can therefore decide to dispose of it otherwise than in a painful self-inflicted way manifesting itself as guilt, depression and moral unease.

The short answer to our question is that identification cannot become conscious to any great extent because it is dynamic – in other words, the product of conflicting forces and attitudes – and, as in the instance just discussed, actually compulsive in its effect. By remaining unconscious the dynamic disposition of the instinctual drives cannot be altered by interference of the ego. In this respect the unconscious is like a read-only memory constituted ultimately by the genes. But anything which undergoes repression also sees its status changed from a read/write, modifiable one to a compulsive, read-only, unmodifiable one. Unalterable and inerasable, whatever is repressed maintains a constant dynamic pressure against the ego which the latter, because of its ignorance of the unconscious, cannot escape.

This realization suggests that consciousness, especially consciousness understood as self-referential, is not purely defensive in the sense of being self-deceptive-in-the-interests-of-deceiving-others. Undoubtedly, as we saw, consciousness does have that function and, as such, may perhaps be visualized rather like a cursor on a computer screen which moves over the pre-conscious field (the latter including all that can become conscious), drawing attention to what we can avow as our own, but away from what we cannot. But equally, it could be regarded as having the other function of a cursor: not merely drawing attention to a part of the program and displaying relevant data, but also focusing attention on points where changes could be made, or new data inserted. On the basis of this analogy the unconscious would be like parts of a program to which the cursor of consciousness could not be returned, and which could not therefore be modified, added to or deleted. Then the fact that some things were beyond the reach of the pre-conscious cursor would not merely be because they were socially unavowable, but alternatively because their adaptive function required that they remain unalterable, or, in psychological terms, *compulsive*.

In this way a dynamic, psychological mechanism could influence behaviour just as effectively as a more directly genetically-encoded determinant, but with much greater flexibility and with the added adaptive advantage which direct gene-determined behaviour could not confer: an ability to interact dynamically with the environment, evidently the chief reason for our more specific adaptive successes, among which nomadic pastoralism must surely be one.

Action and reaction in industrial adolescence

In concluding this study of the role of dynamic identification in promoting human kin altruism, I would like to draw attention to one final strength of the theory which follows directly from the point made at the conclusion of the last section.

It is a notable feature of dynamic theories of human motivation that, analogously with dynamics in physics, they can account, not merely for action, but also for *reaction*. This, a non-dynamic, deterministic theory cannot do. Cultural determinism tends to treat individual reactions against it as evidence for the omnipotence of cultural conditioning rather than the contrary and consigns such behaviour to residual, catch-all categories such as 'deviance', 'egoism', 'alienation', or whatever. Genetic determinism, by contrast, assumes an equally strong and direct link between genetic determinants and behaviour and just ignores what does not fit its rather rough and ready explanations (for instance, most of the facts about incest). However, a genuinely dynamic theory like the one being proposed here allows for reaction against something like identification as well as action in accordance with it. As an example, let us consider the situation with regard to parental investment and parent–offspring conflict in modern, industrial societies.

With the possible exception of primal conflicts occasioned by the beginnings of hunting which we noted earlier, tension between adolescents and adults seems to have reached an unprecedented level in industrial societies. Indeed, the very existence of adolescents as a distinct social stratum with their own culture, manners of dress, speech and so on is practically unknown in previous societies where adolescence, even when culturally marked by something like an age-grade system, is really only a transitionary period between childhood and adult life. Furthermore, in some societies, notably the most primitive like those of the Australian aborigines, adolescence as such hardly exists. Because of the importance of the institution of initiation, individuals quite literally go from being children to being adults in just a few days or weeks, depending on how long initiation lasts. There is no culturally-recognized or psychologically significant transitionary status apart from this.[45]

A greater contrast with industrial societies could hardly be imagined. In the latter case adolescence seems to begin earlier and earlier as higher standards of nutrition trigger puberty at progressively younger ages (because puberty seems to be weight-dependent). The demands of formal education and economic pressures on young people operate to lengthen the period at the other extreme, causing some to postpone marriage and the achievement of an economically self-supporting status until well into their twenties. The net result is a very long adolescence in which many young people occupy an intermediate status between childhood and maturity often lasting a decade or more.

Yet industrial adolescence is not merely lengthened out of all proportion, it is also the occasion for conflict with parents, parental values and with the general ambient adult culture which causes youth to become practically synonymous with protest, conflict and a general rejection and revolt against anything stigmatized as 'traditional', 'establishment' or 'normal'. In their political heroes, their attitudes, their music and the 'youth-culture' in general young people seem to express feelings which are often complex and even self-contradictory but which always seem to involve conflict with parental authority. Indeed, so severe have these conflicts become that nowadays some element of protest, defiance and confrontation with adults is regarded as normal for the adolescent and is certainly institutionalized in the modern cultural mythology.

In no previous culture in history have young people been such an unmistakable and significant cultural group, been so distinctively dressed and differently behaved, been so vociferously vocal in protest against parental values and have so openly confronted the general culture as a 'problem'. If modern social scientists of the cultural-determinist schools can be justly criticized for overlooking child–parent conflict in childhood, not even they can be accused of failing to notice it in adolescence. So obvious has it become that, far from

[45] For a fuller discussion of aboriginal adolescence see Badcock, *Madness and Modernity*, pp. 32–4.

being impressed by its significance, we are in danger of taking it for granted, of failing to see just how exceptional and unprecedented it is and of misunderstanding it because we imagine for some reason that it is 'natural', and only to be expected.

If, accepting that parent–child conflict does seem to have become chronic during adolescence in our culture and even severe in many cases, we now look for causes, I think that we must be prepared for a surprise. It would certainly be a mistake to take a too-simple view of the matter and merely regard such modern antagonisms as repetitions of primal father–son conflicts as may have occurred at the dawn of culture. There is perhaps such a dimension to the problem,[46] but if we are looking for causes we might do worse than to begin by considering whether there is not something distinctive of the modern industrial family which might throw some light on the question of adolescence.

If we agree with a number of other well-informed commentators that modern 'youth culture' is distinguished by its *oppositional* style[47] and accept that what is being opposed here is mainly parental, 'establishment', and traditional values, then it might be worth wondering what occasions this opposition, this protest, this reiterated longing to be free. 'Free of what?', we might ask.

If such an adolescent protest was caused by genuine repression and exploitation of adolescents then it ought to have broken out in the past, when very many adolescents of all but the most affluent classes were widely employed as domestic servants, apprentices and sometimes even as prostitutes. Such young people, often exploited with what one social historian calls 'almost limitless sadism from their masters'[48] had every cause to revolt against such treatment; yet the fact is that the great age of adolescent protest does not coincide with one of ruthless exploitation of the young but with one of unprecedented freedom, affluence and opportunity.

[46] Badcock, *Madness and Modernity*, chapters 3 and 5.
[47] See especially B. Martin, *A Sociology of Contemporary Change*, p. 150.
[48] L. Stone, *The Family, Sex and Marriage in England, 1500–1800*, p. 120.

This strongly suggests that if we are looking for the origin of the protest in simple causes we shall certainly be disappointed.

A more promising line of inquiry might be to wonder whether it was not this very freedom and affluence of the young, possibly coupled with other factors, which made them notably contemptuous of parental values. Such is probably the case; but the fundamental cause will elude us until we succeed in finding a more specific answer to our question: freedom from what?

The answer to this question might be: from the parents and their values, since, as we have seen, that is what is being opposed. Yet this only leads to another question: namely, why, in modern industrial society, should adolescents be so intent on freeing themselves from the parents?

Here the answer probably lies in the unique conditions of family life found in modern societies. In the pre-industrial societies where older, extended family networks of kinship were breaking down it is notable that the phenomenon of extrusion was very marked.[49] Here 'extrusion' is taken to mean any means by which children or adolescents of any age are fostered out to other families, either as employees in the case of servants and apprentices, or as wards sent to live with other families, scholars at boarding school and so on.

If we take employment first, recent studies show that 'in rural Denmark in 1787/1801 well over 50% of those who survived past adolescence were in service at some point in their lives'; and although Danish figures for this period may be on the high side the same study goes on to conclude that 'it was always true that a very substantial proportion of young men and women experienced service at some point in their lives.'[50] Before the industrial revolution in England,

> The fostering-out system by which children were sent away from home at an early age to act as servants or living-in apprentices in someone else's house meant that perhaps two

---

[49] See M. E. Spiro, *Oedipus in the Trobriands*, chapter 6.
[50] J. Hajnal, 'Two Kinds of Pre-industrial Household Formation', in R. Wall, J. Robin and P. Laslett (eds), *Family Forms in Historic Europe*.

out of every three households contained a resident adolescent who was not of the family.[51]

The same author concludes that most upper-class parents, and many middle- and lower-class ones, saw relatively little of their children because of the common practice of 'fostering out'.[52] Furthermore, he makes the reasonable assumption that 'the longer a child lived, the more likely it was that an affective bond would develop between it and its parents.'[53] Given the very high infant mortality rates of the pre-industrial era, the habit of putting out babies to wet-nurses in the more affluent social classes and the pervasive cultural attitudes to family life and children, it does not seem entirely unlikely that parent–child emotional ties were less extensive and less deep than they were to become later. This, combined with extrusion whereby children of the more affluent classes, after being put out to wet-nurses were 'thereafter . . .brought up mainly by nurses, governesses and tutors' and then sent off to boarding school between the ages of seven and thirteen meant that it was not only among the masses that 'census data suggest that from just before puberty until they married some ten years later, about two out of three boys and three out of every four girls were living away from home.'[54]

Following industrialization all this was to change dramatically. In the second half of the twentieth century medical advances had made it a practical certainty that any child born would survive until maturity and effective contraception and safe abortion had meant that the number of children in the family had reduced markedly from the anomalously high levels accompanying the onset of industrialization. Now, with extrusion a rarity and with a new cultural attitude to family life which stressed its emotional closeness and the psychological needs of the child for an adequate parent, it became much more likely that the child–parent bond would

---

[51] Stone, *The Family*, p. 120.
[52] Ibid., p. 83.
[53] Ibid., p. 83.
[54] Ibid., p. 84.

become a strong and profound one. With the further withering of extended-family kinship ties in most social strata and ethnic groups the modern 'nuclear' family, although nothing like as stable or as permanent as some of the older holistic social theories might give one to suppose, nevertheless predominated as the primary milieu for child-rearing, and intense child–parent emotional bonds became the norm for the culture.

I think that it is against this background that modern youth culture and adolescent protest should be seen. Anna Freud once put it very clearly and simply when she expressed it as a case of 'using the hate to counter the love'.[55] In other words, adolescent protest, opposition and the ubiquitous desire to be free might all turn out to be expressions of a need to be free of the parents, to protest against the adolescent's own dependency on them and to oppose the tie of love and dependency with all the hate, aggression and antagonism which the still-insecure young adult can muster. This explains why the only significant targets of student protest are always identifiable with the parents and their values[56] and why it is the need to *protest* rather than to establish some better alternative that chiefly seems to motivate it. The youth counter-culture then may be not so much opposed to adult culture as designed to counter the adolescent's own dependence on the parents – an externalized inner conflict, like so much else in modern adolescence.[57]

In this respect it is probable that the modern fashion for 'permissive' child-rearing has only aggravated the problem further by increasing the dependency of children on parents who yield to them and become willing accomplices to the fulfilment of their wishes. The fact that this also frustrates the children and makes them resent their dependency further only complicates the already-difficult task of adolescence and makes final emancipation from reliance on the parents even

[55] Personal communication.
[56] See Badcock, *Madness and Modernity*, pp. 99–102.
[57] Anna Freud, *The Ego and the Mechanisms of Defence*, part IV.

more problematic. When we include in this picture the attempt to hide the libidinal side of the relationship under the permissive excuse which claims that it does not matter and also point out that weak parental figures make inadequate models for adolescent identification and adult-modelling, we have most of the ingredients for the modern adolescent problem.[58]

It may well be a general principle that when resources available for investment in offspring by parents undergo an independent expansion offspring will deploy new tactics in order to solicit the newly available investment. Such certainly seems to be the case where neoteny is concerned because, as we saw earlier, there are reasons for thinking that this form of investment-soliciting regression only became a practical proposition for our species when hunting began, bringing with it home bases at which nursing mothers could be relatively easily provisioned and generally providing the ambience in which the vastly increased level of parental investment which neoteny occasioned could be made.

It seems that the onset of industrialization had a comparable effect in that gross parental investment (at least in surviving children and perhaps especially by the mother) tended to increase, expanding family sizes to anomalously large values. In time, as we have just seen, family sizes adjusted downwards to something like the traditional level. Nevertheless, the fact that any child born was now almost certain to reach adulthood meant that, even though the gross level of parental investment measured in terms of number of pregnancies, duration of child-care and general demands on the parents may have declined somewhat from the unprecedentedly high levels of the nineteenth century, the net level of investment has probably reached unparalleled heights. Both directly through face-to-face parent–child interactions and indirectly through social provision of education, grants and

[58] For a fuller discussion of these points see H. and Y. Lowenfeld, 'Our Permissive Society and the Superego', *The Psychoanalytic Quarterly*, 39, 1970.

various kinds of welfare for young people, parental invest-ment in the young – and therefore young people's depen-dency on such investments – has probably never been higher.

Such high levels of investment suggest correspondingly strong or lengthy identifications, perhaps especially by par-ents with their children (as the psychological means of mobi-lizing the altruistic behaviours demanded), but also by children with parents (as the means of soliciting those beha-viours). At the very least, such unprecedented investment might create considerable problems of dependency in its recipients – problems complicated by guilt and gratitude as much as by the desire to be independent and free.

Unlike the situation in primal hunter-gatherer societies, modern societies have no institutionalized initiation rituals to bring about the break and to substitute for childhood identifi-cations (mainly, in primal societies, with the mother) adult ones (mainly in that case with the father). Again, unlike most other non-industrial societies and unlike Western societies before the nineteenth century, the institution of extrusion does not exist to any great extent to weaken and diversify the parent–child tie. Consequently, modern young people, reaching the age at which they should begin to mature into independent adults, seem to find great difficulty in breaking the ties which bind them to dependence on the parents. This leads to the oppositional style of protest and the antagonistic behaviour, bizarre appearance and general 'revolt' of youth.

Here the fundamental need is not to identify with, but to *differentiate from*, the parents, their values and their culture. Differentiation means all the things we find: emphasis on being different, on being independent, on being oneself, on breaking away. It leads to a form of behaviour whose very exaggeration, compulsiveness and one-sidedness betrays its essentially *reactive* nature. Where identifications are apparent they are usually with hero-figures, ideals and values which contradict those of the parents and their world – counter-identifications, in fact.

In summary then, we may conclude that it is the very significance and strength of infantile ties and identifications with the parents which result in many modern adolescents making such a fetish of their reaction against them and emphasizing their independence in such exaggerated and compulsive ways. Only a genuinely dynamic theory of human nature could explain such perverse, contradictory behaviour and no other theory could possibly hope to relate such apparently egocentric, counter-parental protest to the genetically-determined basis of what appears to be the exact opposite: human kin altruism expressed through dynamic identification. Such apparently perverse, dynamic reversals may come as a surprise to the more simple-minded biological and cultural determinists, but they have long been familiar to psychoanalysis and constitute one of the most important principles of Freudian psycho-dynamics: to just about every psychological action there can be, and often is, an equal and opposite reaction.

3

Induced Altruism, Differentiation and Sadism

The third fundamental form of altruism

So far we have examined two fundamental forms of altruism: kin altruism and reciprocal altruism. We saw that the concept of inclusive fitness in the first case, and reciprocal benefit in the second, explained the altruistic behaviours in question in a manner which was quite satisfactory to genuine Darwinism and indeed provided many new and significant insights. The time has now come to mention the third fundamental form of altruism as it is found in the biological world.

This is what we might term 'induced' or 'obligatory' altruism. It will not qualify as altruism under the conventional, subjective philosophical meaning of the term, but it most certainly will do if we define it in terms of the objective definition of altruism currently in use in biology. This, as we saw earlier, defines an altruistic act as one in which the donor promotes the fitness of the recipient at the donor's expense. If the altruism benefits a set of the donor's genes present in the recipient we are dealing with a case of kin altruism; if the donor receives some subsequent benefit from the recipient of the original altruistic act we are talking about reciprocal altruism.

But what of an initial reciprocal exchange in which there is no return to the original altruist? Is this not still altruism? Consider an example, the one I referred to earlier, of the false cleaner which, instead of doing a service for the grouper on the coral reef by cleaning its gills and so on, takes a bite out of it and makes off. On our objective definition of altruism the grouper has undoubtedly performed an altruistic act, albeit an induced or obligatory one, because it has enhanced the fitness of the predatory cleaner by providing it with a meal. But the fact that the grouper was deceived makes no difference as far as the altruism of his side of the bargain is concerned – however we look at it the grouper undeniably provided a service for the false cleaner which represented in this case a very real and tangible cost, one which can easily be imagined to have reduced that particular grouper's Darwinian fitness quite measurably (since it is not unreasonable to assume that injured and bleeding fish on average leave fewer descendants than healthy ones). It seems that we are forced to conclude that *whenever one organism promotes the fitness of another at its own expense and without reciprocal benefit to itself or benefit to its genes present in the recipient it has perforce performed an act of induced altruism.*

It might also seem that, as far as biology is concerned, there are some grounds for the proposition that induced altruism could safely be ignored – after all, it is merely another name for something which is perhaps better described as the opposite of altruism, namely, *selfishness*, because the actor receives a benefit to himself whilst inflicting a cost on another. In my example of the false cleaner we can clearly see that however it may be represented as induced altruism from the point of view of the prey – for that is what the grouper was – it was an act of archetypical selfishness on the part of the predator. Indeed, strictly speaking, predation must overlap the concept of induced altruism because, even though the prey actively attempts to avoid contributing to the fitness of the predator, the fact that it ineluctably does so qualifies its sacrifice as in some sense altruistic if we have already defined altruism by its objective consequences, not its subjective intention. To be exact: *induced altruism describes selfishness from the point of view of the exploited party*. This may not be our conventional way of looking at things, but, as I

E

hope to be able to show quite shortly, it is a way of looking at things logically unavoidable in biology and psychologically essential if we are to understand the much-vaunted 'pure' altruism of the human race.

One advantage of the theory of induced altruism is that it neatly maps onto one of the most fundamental and important mathematical models for cooperative behaviour, the so-called 'Prisoner's Dilemma'. This portrays social interaction in terms of the following archetypical microcosm. Imagine two prisoners, arrested for some crime of which they are innocent. Their captors are offering a reward to anyone implicating the guilty party. The prisoners are held in isolation and told the same thing: whoever implicates the other in the crime will go free and receive the reward, while the other will serve a long sentence. If both maintain their innocence, both will be released. However, if both implicate each other, both will serve sentences, although shorter than if only one is punished.

Clearly, our prisoners are in a real dilemma. Both have an incentive to cooperate with each other in maintaining their collective innocence. But, at the same time, each knows that he has a considerable incentive to defect and claim the reward for himself. Unfortunately, he also knows that the same incentive to defect exists for his partner, and that if he cooperates while his partner defects he will suffer the worst penalty. On the other hand, if they both defect and claim the reward neither will get it but both will suffer a penalty.[1]

What is contained here is the basic situation with regard to reciprocal and induced altruism (kin altruism does not figure as such[2]). Defection – incriminating the other – amounts to selfishness since it is motivated by the desire to win the

---

[1] If we call the temptation to defect T, we might term the corresponding sucker's payoff S; if R is the reward for mutual cooperation and P the payoff for mutual defection, we have the quantitive relation $T > R > P > S$. We also assume that the incentive to cooperate is greater than the average payoff from successful defection and unsuccessful cooperation, i.e., $R > (T + S)/2$. (After R. Axelrod, *The Evolution of Cooperation*.)

[2] Although see Hamilton and Axelrod in *ibid*.

reward for the defector. However, this can only come about by inflicting the worst penalty on the other. If both defect, then both bear the cost of mutual selfishness – each loses the freedom which both would have won if they had both cooperated. If both cooperate by not implicating the other, both gain, but only by reciprocating their non-implication. This is the equivalent of reciprocal altruism because the sacrifice of each (forgoing the reward) results in the reciprocal benefit of freedom for both.

If one cooperates and the other defects, the cooperator has effectively performed an act of induced altruism – the corollary, as we have seen, of the defector's selfish gain. If we accept that mutual cooperation in Prisoner's Dilemma models reciprocal altruism, then I can see no alternative to seeing defection by one party and cooperation by the other as equally implying an act of altruism on the part of the co-operator since, by definition, altruism is being seen purely in terms of its objective consequences, and by not defecting and acting selfishly the cooperator must be acting altruistically. The beauty of Prisoner's Dilemma – one of its many beauties – is that this objective, consequential nature of cooperative altruism clearly implies the notion of induced altruism in circumstances where the behaviour is identical with that in reciprocal altruism – cooperating – but the outcome only different because of what the other party did independently (defected). However one looks at it, induced altruism seems an inevitable category in any general theory of altruism.

As far as predation is concerned, the selfish gain to the predator represents an enforced and obligatory sacrifice on the part of the prey which must logically qualify as objectively altruistic in its consequence since it benefits the predator at the prey's expense (in terms of Prisoner's Dilemma the prey *has* to cooperate while the predator defects). So one-sided is this benefit that if predation were the only known instance of induced altruism we should be perfectly justified in ignoring the concept as largely redundant and of no significant use. Nevertheless, the form of social predation called *enslavement*, found in numerous ant species and among human beings, indicates that the notion of one individual being compelled to promote the fitness of another at his own expense is by no means perverse since in the ant case the slaves perform exactly the same activities which, were they to belong to the host species, would be regarded as expressions of kin altruism. What I am arguing is that the parasitized form of altruism found in this case should be regarded as part of a very much larger and more general category: that of induced altruism.[3]

If we turn our attention to parasitism, we shall immediately see that, because the situation is not as one-sided as it is in the case of predation, it makes perfectly good sense to talk of the host as providing something for the parasite and of the parasite as deriving some benefit from the host which is objectively altruistic as far as the host is concerned. Admittedly, some instances of parasitism seem little different from predation; yet in others the cost and benefit calculations are complex and point to the relevance of regarding parasitism as a case of induced altruism. A tape-worm seems a rather uninteresting parasite from this point of view because its parasitism is a sort of mild and chronic predation, one that does not kill the host outright, but may weaken it. Gut bacteria, on the other hand, may also qualify as parasitic because, like the tape-worm, they eat matter found in the intestines; but, unlike the worm, they may also contribute positively to the good of their host in aiding in the digestion of food. Indeed, some cases of parasitism in which such reciprocal benefits are even more finely balanced may qualify as mutualism or symbiosis, and in these cases the concept of reciprocal altruism is certainly relevant. The acacia tree which supplies food specifically manufactured for its host species of ant can hardly be seen as parasitized by the latter

[3] P. van den Berghe follows a comparable, if more limited, line of reasoning in his *Human Family Systems*, where he distinguishes between kin selection, reciprocity and 'collective coercion for purposes of intraspecific parasitism' (p. 15).

when the ants return the benefit by attacking animals which attempt to browse on its leaves and even weed the ground around it to keep it free of competition from other trees. In such examples as these cooperation has evolved into a permanent and fundamental relationship between the species concerned.

It is in the context of a discussion of social parasitism that Robert Trivers has independently introduced the term 'induced altruism'. Following a discussion of kin and reciprocal altruism he adds that

> A third way in which altruism may be selected is through parasitism. The recipient *induces* altruism that would normally be directed elsewhere or not displayed at all. Perhaps the best-known examples are the brood parasites of birds, species whose members are wholly specialized to lay their eggs in the nests of other birds so the hatchlings will be reared to independence by them.[4]

In this case the parasitism in question is certainly significant and the altruism of the exploited party very obvious. Raising the progeny of another species involves considerable parental investment by the hosts which would not come about unless they had been deceived by skilful mimicry of their own eggs on the part of those of the brood parasite. Again, the fact that it is a deception which has motivated the altruistic act in no way alters its objective consequence; the fact that it does not promote the inclusive fitness of the hosts is an accident resulting from a misidentification of kinship. It in no way alters their behaviour, which is still as objectively altruistic as it was when it was performed on behalf of their own offspring. Only if we persist in thinking in terms of subjective intention does it make any difference; but who would seriously propose that the subjective altruistic intentions of the birds in question should be taken into account? If we take the reasonable view that altruism can only be inferred from behaviour, then we have no real alternative but

[4] R. Trivers, *Social Evolution*, p. 49.

to follow the line of reasoning being pursued here and ignore the error in the birds' subjectivity as irrelevant to the objective nature of their altruism. (In this case the defection of the parasites is as obvious and indeed literal as the cooperation of the hosts.)

Another example of parasitic manipulation and exploitation is the liver fluke which infests sheep. One of the most interesting things about the complex life cycle of the liver fluke is that it gets into the sheep via ants which come into contact with fluke-infected sheep faeces on the ground. Once inside the ant's body, the presence of the liver fluke causes the ant to modify its behaviour in such a way that it climbs to the end of a blade of grass and waits there, to be eaten by a sheep. In behaving in this way the ant is clearly being manipulated by the liver fluke (in fact by a liver fluke 'brain-worm' which attacks the ant's central nervous system) and is quite unmistakably performing an act of altruism, albeit of the induced kind.

In this example the liver fluke which differentiates into the brain-worm and thereby modifies the ant's behaviour itself perishes when the ant is eaten. This occurrence is probably to be interpreted as a case of kin altruism because it is likely that the liver fluke concerned is closely related, perhaps even genetically identical to those which eventually infect the sheep.[5] But if we are justified in invoking kin altruism to explain the self-sacrifice of the brain-worm I do not see how we cannot be allowed to invoke induced altruism to explain the exactly comparable self-sacrifice of the ant. In both cases an organism, be it brain-worm or ant, sacrifices itself for the benefit of the liver fluke cells which will eventually infect a new sheep. The fact that the brain-worm is presumably

[5] This case has also been one which is claimed to indicate group selection, with the group of liver fluke cells inside the ant perpetuating itself in this way. However, the conditions for such trait-group selection seem to resemble so closely those relating to kin selection that the use of the theory in this case seems of doubtful value. It would only be compelling if the liver fluke cells in question were genetically disparate – an unlikely circumstance. For a further discussion, see D. Barash, *Sociobiology and Behaviour*, pp. 112–15, and Trivers, *Social Evolution*, p. 63.

genetically programmed to do so and the ant presumably manipulated by the brain-worm's interference in its central nervous system seems neither here nor there as far as the basic logic of the situation is concerned. In both cases ultimate altruism – self-sacrifice – occurs; in one we are justified in all probability of speaking of kin altruism, in the other I can see no alternative to regarding it as a paradigmatic case of induced altruism. Furthermore, and as we have already seen in my stock example of the exploited grouper and predatory cleaner fish, it seems that every instance of non-reciprocation must qualify as induced altruism if it is not explicable as one of kin altruism.

Putting crude coercion as found in predation and enslavement on one side for a moment, it seems that if induced altruism were ever to evolve as a significant form of altruism it would have to do so as a subtle extension of parasitism, manipulation and exploitation. But manipulation and exploitation of what? The foregoing examples show that, at least in animal populations, what we are calling induced altruism is usually a kind of parasitism of other, more regular kinds of altruism. In particular, we might expect to see it evolve as a perversion of kin altruism (as in brood parasitism) or reciprocal altruism (as in my original example of the false cleaner). As Trivers points out,

> Although parasitized altruism is really a form of selfish behaviour, the actor being the recipient of the altruism, we should note that all systems of altruism are vulnerable to parasitisms in which individuals pretend to a degree of relatedness they do not possess or a degree of reciprocity they will not express.[6]

Assuming this to be the case, we might draw up a list of conditions favouring the evolution of induced altruism in the majority of cases:

1 Conditions in which disparity of access to coercion or its successful use make it possible for one organism to induce

[6] Trivers, *Social Evolution*, pp. 52–3.

a sacrifice in another to its own advantage (e.g., predation and enslavement), but also including those favouring indirect, remote or covert coercion, manipulation or control (e.g., the liver fluke brain-worm).

2 Situations in which elaborate systems of communication are available, allowing plenty of scope for dissimulation, counterfeit and general misrepresentation (especially regarding kinship or reciprocity) (e.g., brood-parasitism); or alternatively, in which impoverishment of perception of less elaborate information has the same result (e.g., cuckoldry based on uncertainty of paternity).

3 Circumstances where altruistic acts can become parasitized, redirected, generalized or detached from specific adaptive behaviours such as those relating to kin or reciprocal altruism, indeed, in which altruism itself might become characterized by its generality, arbitrariness, abstraction and 'purity' (e.g., much of what passes as human altruism).

4 Circumstances of differentiation of behaviour, skill or competence, life-style or social groupings in which the differential costs and benefits of altruistic acts will encourage differential inducement (e.g., parental efforts to induce altruism in offspring beyond what the offspring themselves would wish).

5 Finally, perhaps as an extension of a pre-existing tendency to elaborate reciprocal altruism since all non-reciprocated acts of altruism not definable as kin altruism qualify as instances of induced altruism and might bring in their train exactly the evolutionary consequences outlined above – the evolution of a complex psychological system culminating, perhaps, in a differentiation of consciousness (because a lack of awareness of one's own selfish gain from other's acts of altruism would contribute to the efficacy of one's advocacy of their altruism).

Of these conditions, several are interconnected because, for instance, a pre-existing system of reciprocal altruism would predispose an organism to evolve complex communicative means which might be a precondition, along with the differentiation of consciousness, of a tendency to generalization of altruistic behaviour. Many of these conditions apply with special force and relevance to modern human beings and so it is perhaps not surprising that it is in the modern human context that the theory of induced altruism really comes into its own.

Indeed, if we were prepared to take it seriously we might begin to wonder about the extent to which a list of attributes which many would regard as distinctively human was not in large part a consequence of these five principles: for example, condition 1 above, subtle and blatant coercion, might be seen as corresponding to *government* and *politics* in general; 2, complex and corruptible communication, might suggest *language* and cultural codes such as music, literature and other forms of artistic representation (which, in their exploitation of the emotions and the unconscious would also cover circumstances of impoverishment of information); 3, generalization and detachment of altruism, might similarly suggest *morality* and *ethical codes* as I have already hinted; 4, social differentiation, inevitably calls to mind *social structure*, especially the division of labour and social stratification; finally, 5, pre-existing reciprocal altruism, might suggest the all-important role of *trade* and *economic exchange* in all human societies.

Perhaps this is not an exhaustive list of the distinctively human; but take language, music, art and literature, morality, social structure, government and the economy away and one cannot help feeling that the greater part of what is peculiar to our species has vanished. Certainly, linguistics, literary and artistic criticism, philosophy, sociology, political science, economics, psychoanalysis in particular and psychology in general[7] would all seem studies of the distinctively

---

[7] The latter two corresponding to the importance previously noted of repression and other psychological mechanisms in human reciprocal interactions.

human and, with the possible exception of the first (linguistics), would all seem to display that controversial, far-too-socially-and-personally relevant character which makes progress in these studies so difficult, so often opposed, and so evidently subject to prejudice and subjectivism of all kinds. Indeed, given the intrinsically predatory, exploitative and dishonest nature of the more imaginative and perhaps characteristically human forms of induced altruism, one should perhaps expect a hundred false insights to cloud every true one in these fields which so intimately touch on human nature.

Language, untruth and evolutionary logic

I suspect that there is a widely held prejudice which assumes that all the very evident short-comings of human languages, their imprecision, ambiguity, redundancy and general impression of arbitrariness and disorganization when compared with their man-made equivalents employed in computing, communications or mathematical logic, results from the fact that human languages are natural. We probably assume – probably for reasons not unconnected with the matter in hand – that if something is natural it is less likely to be logical, mathematical or precise, as opposed to something which we have devised ourselves as an artefact of culture. Nature, after all, is supposed to be red in tooth and claw, not well-read in mathematical logic.

Yet the moment we come to think about it, we will immediately see that this really is nothing more than prejudice, for no one can deny that it is precisely because nature is mathematical, precise and organized that human logic, scientific method and mathematical description have been able to comprehend it. Of course, there is still the lingering feeling that, even though such must be the case, living matter is somehow partly exempt. I suspect that we tend to see the biological world as half-way between the purely physical world which does obey complex but relatively precise mathematical laws, and the cultural world which does not. However, we have only to contemplate the near-perfect symmetry of the hexagonal lattices produced by honey bees or the immaculate logarithmic growth-spirals seen in many plant and animal structures to realize that this is hardly true even of the biological world. Even the concept of inclusive fitness, we should recall, is amenable to quantitative formulation; and if we consider for a moment the immense information-processing capacity of our own nervous systems, the complex computational routines now known to underlie even simple perceptual processes like colour vision, we will, I think, have to admit that if mere machines are capable of exact logical functioning then there is absolutely no reason why human beings should not be capable of it too.

Admittedly, human languages have evolved to describe a complex and sometimes unpredictable world in which the very fact of signification produces a gulf between the reality signified and the sign signifying it which may easily not be correctly bridged. Furthermore, the fact that they are rich, open-ended systems multiplies the possibility of error, confusion and misunderstanding. Yet the fact remains that even the inevitable degradation of information encountered in man-made communications can often be rectified by relatively simple computational procedures (for example, in retrieving lost information in data relayed from deep-space probes or correcting inevitable memory losses in computer information-storage). If the relatively crude capabilities of modern technology can restore degraded information to something like its original state one wonders why the human brain, with its vaster information-processing potential, could not be capable (and perhaps is capable) of something similar. Finally, it is worth pointing out that if the conveying of correct information were the only function of human communications and if their complexity and open-endedness hindered them in this they would have no alternative but to become simpler and more organized, since the contrary could have conveyed no information and its loss would therefore confer no cost.

In short, I think that we are forced to conclude that if human languages are notable for their high levels of redundancy, semantic imprecision, ambiguity and general lack of logical rigour it is not because they could not have evolved to be otherwise. On the contrary, I think that we must recognize that they are this way for some good evolutionary reason and that, even though human beings could have evolved means of communication comparable to the purest mathematical logic, they have not done so, not because it was impossible, but because it was not adaptive to do so.

The question then becomes: why should interpersonal communications, of which the richest and most important occur through the medium of language, be as they are? Why do they not function more efficiently in their self-evident role as avenues of communication?

The fundamental answer to this question has already been suggested above in my quotation from Trivers where we find him warning us not to assume that animal communication exists solely for the dissemination of truth but to remember that it will often serve an organism's inclusive fitness better as a means of spreading untrue and misleading information. He rightly warns that we should not allow our assumptions about information theory to blind us to the useful evolutionary role of misinformation:

> Verbiage, it may be noted, is virtually defined by its biological inexpensiveness. The difference in cost between true and false statements must be trivial, at least as measured by the energy expended in speaking (compare 'yes' and 'no'), so verbal reality is likely to be a poor guide to social behaviour.[8]

In the previous section of this chapter we noticed that both kin and reciprocal altruism may be parasitized to become what I have termed induced altruism if the communication channels on which the recognition of kinship or reciprocity

[8] Trivers, *Social Evolution*, p. 4.

depends can be subverted. If, like the cuckoo, I can pass my progeny off as someone else's, then I can also pass the considerable cost of raising them to the hosts. Similarly, if, in a reciprocal exchange, I can cheat so that I gain more than I return, I have likewise induced an act of involuntary altruism in my partner which will presumably promote my fitness. In these kinds of instances exploitation of the fundamental forms of altruism involved relies on deception, and the deception in turn on misinformation.

If we follow Trivers and make the by-no-means unreasonable assumption that human language evolved originally in large part as a medium of communication for reciprocal altruism, then it is also not unreasonable to suggest that the apparent imperfections of human languages as far as logical consistency, semantic precision and redundancy are concerned may all reflect not merely the need for this means of communication to convey information, but also its usefulness in communicating misinformation. Furthermore, some of the features in question – notably redundancy, for instance – may reflect another important feature of the system: the need to detect misinformation and to evaluate the reliability of the message. In modern information technology redundancy is built into systems mainly as a means of safeguarding against loss of information or errors in processing. In human languages the very high degree of redundancy seen at all levels (and amplified by attendant features such as gestures, facial expressions and context) almost certainly reflects the same requirement: the need to safeguard against errors and deception in communications which will put the recipient or the sender at a disadvantage.

Correspondingly, the very existence of means to detect misinformation will encourage more effort in hiding it, and here too redundancy may play a part. The repetition of a piece of information may well promote its likelihood of being accepted as genuine, even if it is a piece of misinformation. (Although this may, in its turn, be used as a means of detection: excessive repetition may warn the recipient of the message that it is being over-sold and make them suspicious of it – this sort of competitive out-flanking is referred to as an 'arms race' by biologists, and I think that we can clearly see why.)

One unexpected spin-off from this approach to the evolutionary basis of language is that it suggests a theory about how, in a world in which no music could originally have existed, human beings might nevertheless have evolved a means of appreciating it. This is because it may well be that, just as we now know that many basic perceptual mechanisms are carried out piecemeal in highly specialized regions of the brain (for instance, facial recognition), so evolution put a premium on the development of specialized perceptual abilities regarding the purely acoustic aspects of speech. This is because the detection of misinformation in what someone else is saying may not only be possible by semantic and intellectual analysis addressed to the meaning of their remarks. Individuals often give away a lot about what they really mean by other sensory cues associated, for instance, with the speed, rhythm, pitch, tone and general acoustic nature of their speech. Linguists suggestively speak of the 'tune' of a sentence and common experience shows that a person who, for instance, is depressed will speak more slowly, with less dynamic intonation and with a different acoustic pattern compared with someone feeling elated or excited. Again, a person who is not sure of the value of what they are saying or is actually perpetrating an untruth may give it away by subtle cues relating to the purely 'musical' aspects of what they say. Once a part of the brain specialized to perceive these auditory parameters of speech it was effectively pre-adapted for the appreciation of music. It is presumably because the processing in question takes place at a wholly unconscious, non-semantic level that the perceptual mechanisms concerned can only communicate their findings to consciousness through the regular means by which it perceives inner, subjective processes: through indistinct but significant emotions, intuitions and feelings – the very things which are communicated to us (or so we suppose) by music.

Language, then, may well reflect complex, even contradictory requirements which explain its apparent short-comings. Its semantic imprecision and general ambiguity, so distressing from the point of view of the accurate communication of information, may well be an adaptation aimed at its role as a means of misinformation and, in all probability, as a counter to it (because ambiguity may be exploited to reveal error, as well as to hide it). No politician, advertising copy-writer, door-step salesman or sociologist needs to be told that words are deliciously vague and can be redefined almost without limit if only one is resourceful enough. Indeed, they can even be coined for the purpose as in the case of jargon or they can be reduced to almost complete objective meaninglessness as evidenced by some of the most popular political terminology such as 'equality', 'freedom', 'national interest', 'democracy' and the like. As everyone knows, all slogans are equally meaningful, but some are more equal than others.

Nietzsche's Principle

One of the main concerns of philosophy, and especially of moral philosophy, is the question of general, universal truths. Undoubtedly the quest for these truths sometimes has an objective foundation, as the development of science and mathematics clearly proves. But the question of moral and ethical universals is more controversial and has never been satisfactorily settled, however much some philosophers may have wished that it had been. Yet it may well be that the philosophical pursuit of general moral principles and allegedly universal axioms of morality is, in part at least, only a linguistic expression of one of my postulated conditions for the evolution of induced altruism: conditions favouring generalization of altruism away from specific altruistic behaviours. This capacity for generalization might then be seen as a development of another condition, elaborate systems of information and misinformation, and perhaps as developing especially extensively in the context of abstract concepts like morality and ethics which as abstractions can only be elaborated in purely linguistic terms.

An immediate and obvious application of the generalizing tendency of language in its misinformative aspects is to be seen in its ability to hide and disguise individual and egoistic concerns. I may be consciously or unconsciously (preferably unconsciously in this instance) motivated to do something for my selfish reasons, but if I can present it as some social, generalized, purely altruistic concern then I will probably benefit. In part this will come about because, thanks to the complex psychological system controlling human altruism, individuals are likely to be sensitive to being used by others (that is, to performing acts of induced altruism). But if the individual concerned cannot divine my selfish interest (perhaps because I have become unaware of it myself) they are much less likely to resist my blandishments. On the contrary, this display of altruism on my part may contribute positively by making them feel guilty if they allow their self-interest to stand in the way of my enterprise. It is not difficult to see that if I am particularly desensitized to my own selfishness and have over-compensated by becoming effective in my role as altruist I may be able to shame others into compliance with my wishes – which may well be presented in a further refinement not as *my* wishes, but *theirs*.

Here the generalizing nature of abstract terms such as morality, subjective altruism and 'goodness' serves as a linguistic equivalent of noise in information theory. It is a kind of semantic jamming, a fog of confusion and generality which swamps the hidden signal: my specific, tangible, personal interest. It is almost as if, scanned by the ever-watchful psychological defences of other people, I deployed my own psycho-linguistic counter-measures which, just like their electronic equivalents in modern warfare, seek to confuse, desensitize and outwit the enemy by deception and subterfuge.

But vague, impersonal generalities and ethical euphemisms can be put to even better use outside specific contexts whose very specificity works against the basic generalizing tactic (as when students start getting concerned about the educational value of examinations in their final year). If altruism can be so effectively detached from its specific kin or reciprocal foundations that it can be presented as intrinsically vague, general and divorced from questions of personal motive, then it can be used, not merely to encourage others to go along with it, but as a kind of moral disarmament. This is because it is individuals' self-interest and self-concern which will usually prevent them performing acts of altruism which do not reward those self-interests in some way. The general principle is that acts of induced altruism can only be procured against the resistance of the actors because, by definition, it costs them something to act altruistically. However, if such concern with self-interest can be branded as 'selfish', 'anti-social', 'immoral' or whatever, then individuals called upon to act altruistically might be much more likely to do so.

In a world where individuals must rely on their sense of self-interest, their aggressive drives and their general capacity to look after themselves as defences against being exploited by others, the condemnation of self-interest by others is not to be wondered at. Such self-concern will not usually militate against honest acts of reciprocal altruism because their benefit – assuming they are duly reciprocated – is likely to be clear, even if it is delayed or indirect. Indeed, given that reciprocal altruism is essentially the balanced trading of individual interests against compensating returns, it follows that self-interest is a major motivator of the system and certainly not to be discouraged – at least as long as the parties to the exchange are assumed to act honestly.

However, if one party cheats – that is, attempts to get by without fully reciprocating – they are effectively trying to induce an altruistic sacrifice in the other, and here anything which justifies or hides such non-reciprocation is to be welcomed by the exploiting party. If one can use boguslygeneralized moralisms to shame people into making excuses for their legitimate self-interest the only practical result – and, of course, in the real world it is the practical results which matter – would be a willingness to accept non-reciprocation as evidence of 'public spiritedness', 'altruism' etc. to the evident benefit of those excused the need to reciprocate for the benefits they enjoy. Indeed, given the central importance of reciprocal altruism in human social interaction, it seems highly likely that the prime motivating factor behind general altruistic moralization and the advocacy of allegedly 'pure' altruism is a desire to cheat by demanding altruistic sacrifices on the part of some without compensating reciprocity by others. The fact that this desire may become completely unconscious because repressed is only a mitigating feature in a rather superficial approach to altruism and one, furthermore, which belies the essential claims of allegedly 'pure' altruism to credibility – the question of the purity of its motives and the disinterestedness of its aims.

Consequently, it follows that induced altruism is highly vulnerable to self-interest, at least as it operates in the putative altruists (not in the instigators of their altruism, of course, because it is in their self-interest to induce as much altruism as possible in their victims if they, the instigators, stand to benefit by it). It follows then that the use of generalizing, moralizing inducements to indiscriminate altruism will find individuals' selfish behavioural proclivities a major obstacle, and this may explain why, in all cultures to some extent, but in some to a major extent, generalized altruism is widely advocated – at least for the other (not necessarily for oneself, of course, but the fact that everyone's own self is someone else's other means that everyone is affected in practice).

In the case of kin altruism we have a somewhat comparable case of rewarded self-interest as we might expect to find in honest reciprocity, but the fact that it is one's genes, rather than one's own self, which receive the benefit complicates the situation because genes have no direct way of influencing behaviour in any particular instance. As we have already seen, it seems realistic to conclude that genes for kin altruism merely predispose human beings to form identifications on the once-sound assumption that such subjective feelings of identity would usually reflect objective genetic kinship. Here self-interest might work against the more obviously masochistic identifications, but probably not to any very great extent against less perverse ones.

However, in the instigator of induced altruism based on identification and the parasitism of kin altruism, the same general principles apply which we noticed in the case of exploited reciprocity. This is because it may well pay exploiters of other people to portray themselves as kin, either by direct and actual misrepresentation of familial relationships (a more common ploy perhaps in kin-based primitive societies than in modern ones), or by indirect, symbolic means which aim to exploit the psychological mechanisms of identification and narcissistic projection. Thus unrelated individuals may portray themselves as 'brothers' or 'sisters' (and stress the identification by pointing to a shared ego ideal as in 'brothers in Christ' or 'sisters in the struggle'); alternatively, exploiters of others' sacrifices from a superior position may style themselves 'fathers' or 'mothers' and their subordinates their 'children', 'sons' and 'daughters'. Any kind of spurious or true family history, genealogy, ethnic or racial myth, religious or political ideology may be pressed into service to secure the identifications in question and to lay the psychological foundation for the parasitized kin altruism which such instances of induced altruism reveal. The cuckoos, it seems, only made a very crude beginning.

One consequence of these insights is that we can immediately see how apparently 'pure' altruism, and, indeed, systems of human ethics in general, might evolve along classical

Darwinian lines. If other people's altruism can benefit me merely because it limits their selfish pursuit of their own interests and generally puts them at a competitive disadvantage in the struggle for existence, it is not difficult to understand why I should have an interest in advocating it, or why they too should see some advantage in advocating altruism on my part. It is really not hard to understand that if reciprocity can be perverted by persuading people that they should not expect any compensating return for their sacrifice, altruism might become generally recommended and a concern with personal advantage hypocritically denied as inferior to a concern for the advantages of others which are then somehow regarded as intrinsically more meritorious than one's own. It does not seem to me amazing that a readiness to identify with the unfortunate plight of others might be capitalized on by appeal to identification with common ideals above and beyond the immediate kin group in which that altruistic psychological propensity first evolved. At the very least, this might provide some insight into how what many people regard as the most distinctively human, 'spiritual' or 'ethical' conduct might have evolved and may once and for all break down the last barriers to the application of the principles of modern Darwinism to human beings.

It is usually assumed that, although Darwinism might be able to explain what we might term 'the beast in man' – that is, the propensities of human beings to act selfishly, cruelly or in accordance with basic animal drives – it cannot hope to explain the higher attributes of our species: our alleged free-will, self-consciousness, moral capacities or our potentiality for behaviours which seem resolutely counter-Darwinian, such as 'pure' altruism, asceticism and self-sacrifice in general. Here, we are told, human consciousness transcends mere animal nature and sets us apart, superior, exalted, not subject to natural drives, exempt from the promptings of a natural selection which may well explain the behaviour of animals but which cannot extend to the explanation of civilized behaviour or the values on which it is based.

That things may not be quite so simple or so gratifying to human pride we have already noticed from our brief consideration of the tendency to form unconscious identifications as a dynamic, psychological extension of what almost certainly evolved originally as the foundations of kin altruism in our species and which today probably underlies many instances of apparent 'pure' altruism. We saw that the masochism of self-sacrifice was not inexplicable on Darwinian lines if we recall that masochism is rewarding for masochists and perhaps derived from a tendency to self-sacrifice-through-identification originally evolved for its adaptive advantages in primal societies where it presumably would have promoted altruism directed towards kin. Freudian insights like these complement evolutionary ones once we see that dynamic mechanisms in human psychology can transform basic instinctual patterns (such as that supposed to underlie the tendency to make identifications) into actual behaviours like masochism which, although apparently perverse, turn out on closer examination to be as much in the service of our animal nature as anything else.

Now we can begin to see that even apparently pure, general, ethical altruism, altruism without personal interest, altruism purportedly only motivated by the highest and most abstract philosophical and religious concerns may, in its practical consequences, rebound to the selfish benefit of its advocates and, given the unique opportunities for generalized deception presented by the evolution of human language, become, not so much a manifestation of the sublimely self-sacrificing in human nature, but evidence of the most abjectly self-serving side of our natural disposition.

Fundamentally, this is an inevitable logical consequence of the general theory of altruism: induced altruism is the reciprocal of selfishness, selfishness is the reciprocal of – and therefore, the defence against – induced altruism. Those who would further their selfish interests might be able to do so by means of inducing altruistic self-sacrifice in others; and others whose corresponding self-interest was not to be so used would do best not to be induced to act altruistically, and thus to act self-interestedly. Instigators of altruistic sacrifice in others for their own benefit would gain by portraying altruism as always good and as intrinsically generalized, pure and selfless; those instigated to act altruistically for the benefit of others would do best to resist by emphasizing their self-interest in not acting altruistically, and would certainly have good reasons for questioning the true motives of the instigators of their altruism.

Only the instigators of generalized self-sacrifice in others for their (the instigators', although, in the deception practised, their, the altruists') benefit would have an interest in portraying altruism as never involving such conflicts of interest. Those who might have been tempted to reject the whole idea of induced altruism on the grounds that, strictly speaking, it must overlap with crude predation, will now begin to see that all induced altruism is predatory in the sense discussed here: even the most ethereal and philosophical concepts of altruism are predatory if they genuinely bring about self-sacrifice without compensating gain to the individuals concerned. Since life is fundamentally competitive, it seems that the only conclusion to which we can come is that the general self-sacrifice of some will always benefit the specific self-interests of others, and, since some will always be others to some, *generalized self-sacrifice, like all induced altruism of which it is only an example, is the product, not of altruistic, but selfish motives*:

> A person's virtues are called *good*, not with regard to the effects they produce for him himself, but with regard to the effects we suppose they will produce for us and for society – praise of virtue has always been very little 'selfless', very little 'unegoistic'! For otherwise it must have been seen that virtues (such as industriousness, obedience, chastity, piety, justness) are mostly *injurious* to their possessors . . . If you possess a virtue . . . you are its *victim*! But that is precisely why your neighbour praises your virtue. Praise of the selfless, sacrificing, virtuous – that is to say, of those who do not expend all

their strength and reason on *their own* preservation, evolution, elevation, advancement, amplification of their power, but who live modestly and thoughtlessly, perhaps even indifferently or ironically with regard to themselves – this praise is in any event not a product of the spirit of selflessness! One's 'neighbour' praises selflessness because *he derives advantage from it*![9]

Thus spoke Friedrich Nietzsche in a passage which, along with others in a similar vein, shows that at least to him the principle of induced altruism was horrifyingly clear. In Freudian terms, we might say that Nietzsche's realization was that, since altruism connotes masochism on the part of the altruist and since masochism naturally corresponds to sadism in others, the advocacy of altruism for others may implicitly serve the sadistic interests of the self.

In terms of Prisoner's Dilemma, Nietzsche's Principle boils down to the injunction: always cooperate! 'This interpretation suggests that the best strategy from the point of view of morality is the strategy of unconditional co-operation':

> The problem with this view is that turning the other cheek provides an incentive for the other player to exploit you. Unconditional cooperation can not only hurt you, but it can hurt other innocent bystanders with whom the successful exploiters interact later. Unconditional cooperation tends to spoil the other player; it leaves a burden on the rest of the community to reform the spoiled player, suggesting that reciprocity is a better foundation for morality than is unconditional cooperation.[10]

It seems that however one looks at it, induced altruism – unreciprocated cooperation through deceit, incitement or coercion – is a very poor foundation for genuine morality.

[9] R. J. Hollingdale (ed.), *A Nietzsche Reader,* p. 101. Nietzsche's emphasis.
[10] Axelrod, *The Evolution of Cooperation,* p. 136.

The holism of poverty

In the passage just quoted Nietzsche points out that what is called 'good' is assumed to be good for society as a whole, even if not for the individual concerned; and it would not surprise me to learn that many objected most strongly to the line of argument in the previous section because they thought that it completely ignored this generalized good. It would seem that one could contradict Nietzsche's assertion with the observation that, even if irksome for individuals, generalized altruism benefits everyone and therefore an insistence on looking at it from the point of view only of individuals is both logically flawed and morally objectionable.

However this may be, the earlier discussion of holism should have prepared us for the possibility that things might not be so simple. The assumption that generalized concepts of morality serve the interests of the social whole can be seen as closely analogous to the now completely discredited line of reasoning which held that, in other species at least, altruistic behaviour evolved because it benefited the group. As I argued earlier, this theory of altruism, so apparently obvious and unobjectionable, relied on virtually no evidence, contradicted basic Darwinian assumptions and, as long as it remained dominant, effectively inhibited any real progress in the understanding of social behaviour in other species. In my view, it has had exactly the same consequence in the human case, and the popularity of what we may call the holistic theory of altruism might be explained by Darwinian and Freudian – not to mention Nietzschean – insights into its tendentious use by human beings.

Such insights may be valuable in explaining why such holistic theories exist since, quite apart from problems which beset them in biology, there are exactly comparable difficulties with holism in the human social sciences. Indeed, using reasoning closely analogous to that employed by sociobiologists like Hamilton and Trivers, students of human behaviour have also begun to question the assumption that, in large groups at least, the real interests of the group and those of its members must coincide:

> The widespread view, common throughout the social sciences, that groups tend to further their interests, is . . . unjustified, at least when it is based, as it usually is, on the (sometimes implicit) assumption that groups act in their self-interest because individuals do . . . the customary view that groups of individuals with common interests tend to further those common interests appears to have little if any merit.[11]

The reason for this lies in a consideration of what is sometimes called the 'free-rider' paradox:

> The very fact that the objective or interest is common to or shared by the group entails that the gain from any sacrifice an individual makes to serve this common purpose is shared by everyone in the group . . . the individual in any large group with a common interest will reap only a minute share of the gains from whatever sacrifices the individual makes to achieve this common interest. Since any gain goes to every-one in the group, those who contribute nothing to the effort will get just as much as those who made a contribution . . . large groups, at least if they are composed of rational indi-viduals, will *not* act in their group interest.[12]

This conclusion, forcefully put forward in the words quoted above from the economist Mancur Olson, is in reality only the equivalent in human terms of the basic Darwinian principle of altruism: since altruism always costs something and since it will benefit some, it pays to enjoy the benefit, but not to pay the cost. Put like this, we can also see it as another version of what, in the context of morality, I have called Nietzsche's Principle. In all these different but related areas it always pays, in Olson's words, 'to let George do it'. In terms

[11] M. Olson, *The Logic of Collective Action*, p. 2.
[12] M. Olson, *The Rise and Decline of Nations*, p. 18.

of Prisoner's Dilemma, it is a question of the payoff for cooperation becoming so diluted in a large group that the temptation to defect becomes very great indeed. The free-rider is the one who defects while the sucker – that is, George – cooperates.

As an example of Olson's point, let us take the case of my income tax liability. It may be claimed that it is in my rational self-interest to pay my taxes because I benefit from them, or so it is alleged. Yet I could counter this by pointing out that it is *not* rational in the least since my personal contribution to government spending is completely negligible. My contribution, if it were not made, would not alter anything; no welfare programme or defence measure would suffer because my taxes, in real terms, are such a minute fraction of government expenditure as a whole that they fall below the threshold of detectability (being considerably less, for instance, than daily variations in the value of the nation's gold and currency reserves). Since my contributions, considered in isolation, make not the slightest difference to the provision of the benefits alleged to come from government expenditure, it would be perfectly rational for me to wish not to pay; and this, of course, is why income tax contributions cause such resentment from most people and have to be sanctioned by threats of punishment. The reason why I must be made to pay is not because it would actually make any difference to the real funds available for government expenditure if I did not, but because others could not be induced to pay if I were permitted not to do so and because mass defection from cooperation with the taxation system certainly would be significant.

Because it will always be in other individuals' interest to 'let George do it', large groups, not organized on lines of identification (in which case we are all Georges), will either have to increase the payoff for cooperation artificially or induce it by coercion:

> If the members of a large group rationally seek to maximize
> their personal welfare, they will *not* act to advance their

common or group objectives unless there is coercion to force
them to do so, or unless some separate incentive, distinct
from achievement of the common or group interest, is
offered to the members of the group individually on the
condition that they help bear the cost or burdens involved in
the achievement of the group objectives. Nor will such large
groups form organizations to further their common goals in
the absence of the coercion or the separate incentives just
mentioned. These points hold true even when there is unani-
mous agreement in a group about the common good and the
methods of achieving it. [13]

In short, *'rational, self-interested individuals will not act to achieve
their common or group interests'*[14] unless induced to do so by
some means independent of the ostensible collective interests
of the group.

Besides providing a close parallel in the human social
sciences to the new sociobiological realism about groups
discussed earlier, Olson's insight into the social and economic aspects of what we might term 'the fallacy of holistic
interests' (the belief that groups automatically promote the
interests of their members) of course explains why the fallacy
exists. If George should do it then he should be motivated by
knowing that his and my and all the other members' interests
are the same. Yet the fact of differentiation – the fact that, in
reality, not all interests are the same – means that holistic
social and ethical theories attempt to bring about acts of
induced altruism by deception: they seek to convince George
that he, rather than I, should do it – something clearly in my
interests, but presented as serving those of the group as a
whole, which, of course, includes George. Nevertheless, if
George does do it (and assuming that George and I are not
related, so that there is no question of kin altruism), what he
has done ineluctably is to perform an act of induced altruism.

The essence of the free-rider theorem is this: in large
groups of unrelated individuals an inevitable differentiation

---

[13] Olson, *The Logic of Collective Action*, p. 2.
[14] Ibid., p. 2.

between individual and collective interests will occur resulting in the temptation for individuals to gain the benefit without paying the cost or, alternatively, not to pay the cost for which they will receive no more benefit than anyone else.

Furthermore, as Olson and others have shown from a wealth of empirical material, it seems that, the larger the group, the greater the disparity. Indeed, on the largest scale possible – that of the entire human race – we habitually assume that each state and nation is out for itself. Yet it is more disconcerting to realize that the principle applies with equal force within nation states as well and that, thanks to the free-rider theorem, the rational interests of the state will almost never coincide with those of any particular group or individual contained within it – least of all the government or elected majority, as the following comments by Milton and Rose Friedman make clear:

> We are ruled by a majority, but it is a majority composed of a coalition of minorities representing special interests . . . Each minority may well lose more from measures benefiting other minorities than it gains from measures benefiting itself. Yet no minority has an incentive to be concerned with the *cumulative* effect of the measures passed.[15]

'A government programme,' they point out,

> almost always confers substantial benefits on a relatively small group while at the same time spreading the costs widely (and hence thinly) over the population at large. As a result, the few have a strong incentive to lobby intensively for the program. The many don't bother even to inform themselves about it, let alone to devote money and effort to opposing it. A legislator who believes that the program on net harms the public is caught in an impossible position. A vote against such a program generates concentrated opposition from the few

[15] M. and R. Friedman, *The Tyranny of the Status Quo*, p. 56.

who will benefit from it, but at best only weak and diffused support from the many who will pay for it.[16]

In other words, not merely individuals but whole groups of individuals can attempt to free-ride in relation to other groups. In so far as the free-riders always represent pressure-groups and special interests they stand in relation to the larger national group just as the individual does to much smaller groups.

Of course, as Olson points out, the free-rider theorem applies only weakly, if at all, to really small groups, where individual and collective interests are much more intimately interrelated and where, I would be tempted to add, real group identifications are more likely to develop. Furthermore, the fact of genetic relatedness will affect the situation and will cause us to add to the purely individual self-interests which Olson has in mind the shared evolutionary interests of the genes which related individuals hold in common. In this way what may on occasions look like real altruism from the point of view of the purely individualistic criterion of self-interest used by the economist will appear to the biologist as evidence of the pursuit of self-interest at the most fundamental level – that of the gene.

The psychological fact of identification beyond objective genetic relatedness bears significantly on Olson's observations and provides a mechanism whereby, thanks to identification, individuals can come to see their personal interests and those of the group as coincident. However, this phenomenon is entirely dependent on the extent to which the individuals in the group share a common ego ideal which, because it is held in common and because it is a part of the individual's ego, bridges the otherwise wide gap between personal egoism and group altruism. Since such a process of identification with a shared ego ideal is entirely unconscious and irrational it does not affect the validity of Olson's general principle (which relates to conscious, rational interests) and

[16] Ibid., p. 40.

means that such a coincidence of individual and group advantage can be procured without coercion by the use of a psychological mechanism originally evolved to serve the coincident evolutionary interests of individuals' own genes and the copies of them present in their kin.

Now we can begin to see that it is the very fact of non-coincidence of the rational interests of the individual and the group which make irrational group identifications and holistically-rationalized inducements to altruism so necessary. It seems that it is the fact of social and economic differentiation which underlies the utility of ethical and social theories which stress the exact opposite – that is, social and economic unity, the dogma that the social whole is always something greater, grander and more deterministically significant than its parts and that the rational interests of such groups and the individuals who compose them are one and the same. As we have seen, holistic social theories serve to hide individual, differential interests behind a smoke-screen of alleged collective interests – collective interests which, in reality, are often a disguise for the individual interests of only some of the members.

It seems that group-interest theories of ethics and behaviour, which once sought to explain biology, now have a biological explanation of their own! Like classic Darwinian mechanisms of adaptation they can be shown to promote the selfish interests of those who advocate them.

Nowhere is this to be more readily seen than in societies in which high degrees of social and economic differentiation, along with very large groups, have come into being. In primal hunter-gatherer societies such is not generally the case. In this instance, groups tend to be small, kin-based and largely undifferentiated apart from obvious species-wide differences related to sex (reflected in economic and nurturing roles) and age. In these societies the high degree of genetic relatedness among members of local groups will mean that the principle of kin altruism covers many aspects of social interaction. Not so agricultural societies, where the existence of much larger and much more heterogeneous groupings, along with a disposable and storable economic surplus, means that social differentiation in terms of status, wealth, political and other factors can develop to bizarre proportions. In urban centres in particular, social differentiation will become very marked, encouraged by the dilution of kinship, the division of labour, stark contrasts between rich and poor and the concentration of population at very high densities.

Only such settings as these could explain the otherwise somewhat perplexing phenomenon of ethical and social systems like Christianity or socialism which stress apparently inexplicable levels of altruistic commitment to the welfare of the social whole. Yet the moment we notice that early Christianity, like modern socialism, first found its roots in the fertile soil of urban centres and among members of social groups relatively disadvantaged with regard to the rest of the society, it is not hard to see how such extremes of ethical and social theory might be explained. On the face of it, to advocate going and selling all one has and giving it to the poor might only be expected to appeal to masochists, and such many of the early converts to Christianity, not to mention some of the later saints, evidently were. But the moment we notice that, thanks to the fact of objective differentiation, most of those advocating such altruism on the part of the rich are actually among the poor, no real paradox remains.

In conclusion, we can now begin to see that even the most idealistic altruism is not necessarily inexplicable to the Darwinian-Freudian theory of behaviour once we begin to appreciate the human mind in its full perversity and complication. When we include the social and economic benefits which follow from advocating altruism which causes others to make sacrifices for oneself, the underlying theme of abject, even predatory self-interest becomes clear. Ethics, morality and all kinds of asceticism will blossom forth profusely once large social groupings and differentiation of behaviour, psychology, life-style or social status mean that altruism can have differential consequences and, in particular, can be imposed as a moral obligation on someone else.

Conclusion:

Psychoanalysis, Altruism and Social Structure

The failure of the therapeutic

Despite the widely-held reservations mentioned at the beginning of this book, many would claim – and with good reason – that Freud's psychoanalysis, like Einstein's relativity, constituted one of the most important scientific revolutions of the twentieth century. In his well-known book, *The Structure of Scientific Revolutions*, Thomas Kuhn points out that such upheavals in science are caused by the adoption of new *paradigms*: that is, exemplary scientific achievements which serve to define a field of enquiry, establish its agenda for research and validation and generally organize its conceptual structure.

Freud undoubtedly brought about such a revolution in the last years of the nineteenth century and the first of the twentieth. In this phase of its development psychoanalysis employed a metaphorical view of the unconscious which was quasi-hydraulic. Consciousness was envisaged to be a sort of psychological dam which held back a flood of repressed material threatening to break through and overwhelm it at any moment and which in the case of neurotics did indeed succeed in breaking through in the form of psychopathic symptoms. Like the dream which it resembled in certain respects, the neurotic symptom was seen to be the outcome partly of a repressed wish, struggling to find expression, and partly of a repressing, censoring agency which strove to keep it away from conscious realization. The aim of psychotherapy at this time was primarily (and especially in the early years) devoted to what is called the *cathartic method*: the liberation of the repressed, pathogenic material so that it became accessible to consciousness and could be *abreacted*, or given conscious expression in a way which revealed its unconscious roots. In this way the analysis strove to substitute rational, conscious condemnation of inappropriate wishes for the irrational, unconscious mechanisms of repression and symptom-formation.

Characteristically enough, even anxiety during this phase of Freud's thinking was conceived as a symptom interpretable in terms of what was at that time the paradigmatic neurotic disorder – conversion hysteria. In this type of neurosis a mental conflict expressed itself in somatic symptoms (hence the *conversion*) which, just like the manifest content of a dream, could be interpreted as the outcome of a wish and the product of a repression. In anxiety hysteria (an entity first clearly identified by Freud) the irrational anxiety was itself seen as a sort of conversion of an instinctual drive, so that at this time repressed libido was conceived as transforming itself directly into anxiety.

Later, in the 1920s, Freud was to revise this rather incorrect theory of anxiety and substitute one which was much more obviously in accordance with psychological reality. The fact that he held to it for so long at the beginning of his career is not, I think, to be regarded as evidence of stupidity or lack of psychological insight on his part any more than Einstein's inability to accept the conventional interpretation of the principle of indeterminacy in quantum mechanics is to be seen as evidence of his intellectual short-comings. In both instances I think that the explanation is the same: it is a case of a pre-existing paradigm being so firmly established in the mind of its originator that, for a time in Freud's case but permanently in Einstein's, he is unable to conceive of another way of seeing things.[1]

In the case of Freud the paradigmatic blindness to the real nature of anxiety which was produced by the dazzling light of his particular conceptual revolution was in due course of time to be corrected. That it was corrected is directly attributable to the nature of paradigmatic revolutions and to the fact that, about 1920, he produced a second psychoanalytic paradigm which ushered in what might be termed the era of defence-analysis, by contrast to the more simple cathartic approach which dominated the first twenty-five years of the psychoanalytic movement.

In this second phase the underlying metaphor ceased to be quasi-hydraulic and became instead structural. Now, rather than seeing psychopathology as the consequence of repressing material in the unconscious where it joined itself to the instinctual drives struggling for expression, it was seen as the outcome of structural conflicts, either between psychological agencies (hysteria, obsessional neurosis and what we would now call manic-depressive disorders), or between the psyche and reality (psychosis). These agencies, the id, ego and super-ego, were defined in terms of their functions within the economy of the mind: the id as the wholly unconscious repository of the instinctual drives and elements associated with them repressed from consciousness; the ego as the managerial agency, in contact with the perceptual system, sensitive to innervations from within the body and from the

---

[1] In Einstein's case the reason may be that he, more than anyone else, had reason to hold on to the idea of determinate causality because, in making the vertiginous conceptual leap which produced the theory of relativity, he had had to abandon belief in the *a priori* existence of the two other categories which philosophers like Kant had imagined ruled our perceptions of reality: namely, space and time. Since relativity specifically retains determinate causality (for instance, in clearly separating 'past' and 'future' of particular frames of reference) it is likely that only with great difficulty could Einstein have been expected to abandon a belief which was absolutely fundamental to relativity and the one sure foundation left after space and time as fixed, absolute and non-relative categories had gone forever.

id and responsible for voluntary movement, thought and conscious intent; finally, the superego, a censoring, evaluating part of the ego constituted on the internalized model of authority figures, particularly from early childhood. Here, indeed, was a model of the mind much more differentiated and subtle than that of the first period (and also much further from common-sense understanding – a clear sign of increasing maturity in a paradigm).

Now classical analysis finally appeared. Instead of probing the patient's unconscious for the repressed, pathogenic material and then regarding the main work of analysis as done when it was brought into consciousness, and externalized in the *transference* (the dynamic psychological relation between the analyst and the analysand), psychoanalysis set about something which was much more like a complete dissection of personality by means of analysis of the ego and its mechanisms of defence. As a result, analyses began to take much longer – the few weeks or months of the early period now gave way to analyses lasting several years. The analyst now perfected the essentially reticent method of the mature psychoanalytic technique, abandoning the almost inquisitorial questioning and reliance on suggestion of the earliest period.

Defence-analysis now opened the way for the analysis of children who, because of their inability to free-associate, had not been suitable subjects for the essentially cathartic method of the first period. Now that the mechanisms of defence were understood and the ego as well as the id became a focus of analysis, children's behaviour and defensive responses were open to reliable analytic interpretation. Indeed, at this time Freud could go so far as to say that children, rather than neurotics, were the main subject of psychoanalytic research.[2] (Certainly, it is noticeable how many analysts prominent in this second phase of psychoanalysis had important connections with child-analysis: e.g., Anna Freud, Melanie Klein, John Bowlby, Donald Winnicott etc.)

[2] S. Freud, Preface to Aichorn's *Wayward Youth*, XIX, p. 273.

Finally, as a clear indication of a deep-seated paradigm shift, the theory of anxiety was revised by Freud. Now, in harmony with the structural-conflict analogy which had replaced the original quasi-hydraulic metaphor, anxiety was understood as resulting from the ego's failure to satisfy the drives of the id (neurotic anxiety), the demands of the super-ego (moral anxiety), or the requirements of reality (realistic anxiety). In each case, however, it was no longer transformed libido but was seen as an ego-response to a structural conflict.[3]

Just as Einstein introduced his revolution in physics in two stages, represented first by special and then by general relativity, so Freud was largely responsible for a second paradigmatic change, not just the first and most obvious one. Admittedly, the second is consequential on the first and a development of it, but the innovations involved in the second should not be underestimated just because it happened that Freud himself was responsible for most of them. (The second psychoanalytic revolution might have been more obvious if, shall we say, it had been Anna Freud who, as well as writing *The Ego and the Mechanisms of Defence* and *Normality and Pathology in Childhood*, had also written *The Ego and the Id* and *Group Psychology and the Analysis of the Ego*. In this case she would have been very much more obviously to the second psychoanalytic paradigm what her father had been to the first.)

If this line of reasoning is correct, and if the two distinct phases of psychoanalysis which have existed up to now can really be seen in this way, then it is not impossible that a third paradigm-shift might occur, perhaps one involving a further elaboration in the psychoanalytic topography and further development of its basic concepts.

Certainly, some would argue that some kind of paradigm renewal is as long overdue in psychoanalysis as it is in the wider social sciences; for in many respects both disciplines have undergone a similar decline, if for different reasons.

[3] S. Freud, *New Introductory Lectures on Psychoanalysis*, XXII, pp. 77–8.

Today psychoanalysis, especially in America, its post-war promised land, no longer occupies the place it once did. Recession, inflation and a proliferation of alternative therapies have put classical psychoanalysis in the shade. Today, when, partly thanks to the factors mentioned above, analyses are taking several years in most cases, fewer and fewer patients can afford to undertake a form of psychotherapy which demands attendance four or five times a week and which exacts fees reflective of the orthodox medical image which American analysts in particular have succeeded in projecting. This, along with recent spectacular improvements in drug-therapies for psychological disorders, means that classical analysis may be increasingly reserved only for the training of analysts and for those few who are prepared to pay the debt in time, money and commitment which conventional psychoanalysis demands.[4]

On the purely intellectual front, things are no better. Gone are the heroic, pioneering days of the 1920s and 1930s, when practically every issue of a psychoanalytic journal contained something new and significant, and when psychoanalytic research continued to break new ground. Today, a feeling of routine, even boredom, seems to have set in with genuine innovation hardly ever occurring but instead ephemeral fads and fashions which come and go, often leaving nothing of any significance behind them. Indeed, so sterile is much modern psychoanalytic writing that those innovators who are most enthusiastically lauded as breaking new ground usually turn out to be breaking up the foundations of the discipline, so laboriously and painfully constructed by the pioneers. The effect is not so much that of normal elaboration and validation of the paradigm predicted by Kuhn but a kind of paradigm-erosion in which the great, strategic ideas of psychoanalysis are slowly eroded by aimless, restless and insignificant working-over.

[4] K. R. Eissler, 'Irreverent Remarks about the Present and Future of Psychoanalysis', *International Journal of Psychoanalysis*, 50, 1969, pp. 461–71.

Part of the explanation for this intellectual stultification of psychoanalysis is probably to be found in its relative isolation within psychoanalytic institutes and other special institutions, walled-off from the outside world, and especially from the universities. This perhaps explains why the reader of modern psychoanalytic literature soon gets the impression that psychoanalysts read psychoanalysis, but little else, at least as far as the intellectual elaboration of their subject is concerned. It seems that the institutional, almost sectarian isolation of psychoanalysis is reflected in a corresponding intellectual and scientific isolation.[5]

Perhaps much of the intellectual exhaustion and isolation of modern psychoanalysis is to be explained as the result of an excessively narrow emphasis on the purely clinical, personal role of psychoanalysis. Of course, if psychoanalysis or related psychotherapies are nothing more than the treatment of isolated individuals in the privacy of the consulting room, then the intellectual isolation of the subject might be forgiveable – and this, undoubtedly, is how many, if not most, therapists see it. But it is not the way Freud saw it. He complemented the purely reductive, microscopic concerns of clinical psychoanalysis with wider, macroscopic concerns rather as Einstein complemented the microscopic, reductionistic tendencies of modern quantum mechanics and particle physics with the macroscopic, cosmological dimension of general relativity (a dynamic paradigm also long opposed by a 'steady-state' theory).

This tendency to ignore the wider, cultural dimension of psychopathology and psychotherapy might be termed 'the individualistic fallacy' and contrasted with the 'holistic fallacy' in the social sciences, which tends in the opposite direction. Perhaps, analogously with the case of Einstein,

---

[5] Another manifestation of this same phenomenon of isolation is seen in the way in which psychoanalysts, even when they are a part of other institutions, such as university social science departments, very often maintain extraordinarily effective intellectual barriers between their psychoanalytic knowledge and other, allied fields. One sometimes gets the feeling that it is the proudest boast of the psychoanalyst/psychotherapist that no one knows what they do away from the department!

Freud will eventually come to be seen as having provided another dimension of insight which, although ignored for many years, might ultimately hold the key to future progress in psychoanalysis and perhaps also provide the antidote to the excessive holism of the modern social sciences.

Furthermore, if the notion of a possible third period of psychoanalytic research comparable to the first two and now overdue has any value we can see that the sociobiological theory of repression might play a part in it comparable to that played by ego-psychology in the second, or the original concept of repression in the first. And if we are correct in believing that holistic theories of the steady-state have caused the social sciences to stagnate and that clinical tunnel-vision has vitiated much of modern psychoanalysis, then a sociobiological, dynamic, evolutionary and species-wide analysis may have much to recommend it.

Just as the discovery of the cosmic background radiation[6] did much to rehabilitate general relativity and to undermine the credibility of the steady-state cosmology, so the recent rediscovery of the unconscious by sociobiology may bring about, not merely the final collapse of steady-state social theories, but the rise of a new psychoanalysis, a third Freudian paradigm built on biological foundations originally laid by Darwin but greatly extended and deepened in recent years.

The dynamic theory of the gene–behaviour interface

Quite apart from its other problems, psychoanalysis faces one further difficulty which has not been mentioned until now. The difficulty which I have in mind is that relating to Freud's instinct theories. As is well known, Freud modified

[6] In the mid-sixties two scientists who were not looking for it at the time detected the electro-magnetic echo of the 'big bang' – the explosive singularity with which the universe is thought to have begun and which constituted a powerful empirical refutation of the steady-state cosmological theory which denied that the universe need have a beginning.

his instinct theory a number of times but ended up with one which founded psychoanalytic metapsychology on a pseudo-biological theory of life and death instincts. I call this theory 'pseudo-biological' advisedly because that is precisely what it is. There never was, never has been and probably never will be any *biological* evidence for the existence of antithetical life and death instincts as the ultimate prime movers of nature. These concepts seem to have more to do with metaphysics than metapsychology, and their presence in psychoanalysis strikes me as an embarrassment, at least for any view of the discipline which takes its claims to scientific status seriously.

In practice, this instinct theory is less important than it seems and it is noticeable that most psychoanalysts since Freud have managed to get by perfectly well without it. Such metaphysically-tinged ideas have little if any relevance for clinical practice and theory and even in Freud's own writings on matters of substance seem to have remarkably small significance. For instance, despite making the general claim that the life instincts aim to bind together, whereas death instincts break apart, he was not in practice as much out of step with modern biological views about the role of sexuality in constituting society as, for instance, some more modern writers like the Structuralist, Claude Lévi-Strauss. The latter believes that sexual attraction is the basis of the family and therefore of society,[7] a point of view largely contradicted by the findings of modern biologists which, because of the differential parental investments of the sexes mentioned earlier, lead to the conclusion that 'Sex is an anti-social force in evolution.'[8] Freud held that it is *narcissistic, homosexual,* rather than heterosexual object–libido which is implicated in group-formation, and that sexual attraction to the opposite sex is much more likely to be the origin of conflict and rivalry among members of the same sex than any natural metaphysical binding of the life instinct.

[7] See the opening argument of C. Lévi-Strauss, *Elementary Structures of Kinship*.
[8] E. O. Wilson, *Sociobiology*, p. 314.

Yet, if psychoanalysis is embarrassed by its failure to provide itself with a credible biological foundation, then modern biology ought to be equally embarrassed by its increasingly evident failure to solve what we may term the problem of the gene–behaviour interface. In the case of those species of lower animals which are the only ones apart from man to manifest very high degrees of altruism along with elaborate social behaviour involving caste specialization and so on, there is no significant problem because it is rightly argued that genes must directly code for the social behaviours in question. For instance, breeding experiments with bees suggest that genetic inheritance affects the ability of workers to carry out certain tasks – strong evidence for a direct gene–behaviour linkage.

Unfortunately for the more naïvely or militantly reductionistic biologists, the same does not appear to be the case with human beings. Here the problem seems to be one of tracing the genetic causes of the vastly complex, variable and perverse behaviour of the human race. I do not doubt for one moment that, ultimately, all behaviour has genetic determinants, since it seems likely that anything which an organism does must finally be accounted for by its genes and their interaction with its environment. The real problem lies in trying to show how distinct genetic determinants might underlie specific behaviours in the human case. A successful theory will have to have the following characteristics:

1 It must allow for the existence of specific genetic factors, but
2 must do justice to the complexity of actual behaviour; and
3 must demonstrate the exact causal links between the two.

The major short-coming of many sociobiological explanations of human behaviour to date has been that although they have been insistent on 1, the genetic determinants, they have been very vague about 3, the linkage problem, or, if they have been specific about 3, have usually offended against 2 by vastly oversimplifying actual behaviour.

A typical, but crucial example of oversimplification and crude biological reductionism might be the current sociobiological dogma regarding incest-avoidance. This holds that 'Sibling incest is preculturally avoided by a biopsychical mechanism'[9] which means that 'It is natural – in the full, biological sense – for people to be opposed to brother–sister incest.'[10] The mechanism in question turns on the alleged fact that 'when children are raised together in close domestic proximity during the first six years of life, they are automatically inhibited from full sexual activity'[11] (sic) – which presumably should be taken to mean 'inhibited from full sexual activity *with one another.*'

This theory is based on only two pieces of evidence (drawn from studies of the Israeli *kibbutz* and Chinese *simpua* marriages), both of which have been subject to devastating criticism and re-evaluation by Melford E. Spiro in the concluding chapter of his book, *Oedipus in the Trobriands*. Far from discrediting the Freudian theory, Spiro concludes that 'the only appropriate response to the question, "Is the Oedipus complex universal?" is "How could it possibly not be?"'[12] But rather than dwell on the very evident short-comings of the crude biological theory of incest-avoidance and repeat the trenchant criticisms made by Spiro and many others, let me, by way of summary, propose an alternative theory which will highlight the differences between the uncharacteristically static, deterministic approach of present-day sociobiology to incest-avoidance and the dynamic, interactive theory of the gene–behaviour interface which I am advocating here.

According to this view of the matter, human beings are not biologically programmed to be sexually indifferent to those with whom they are raised as children. On the contrary, human nature is in large part constituted by evolutionary adaptations originally laid down when our hominid ancestors

[9] J. Shepher, *Incest: A Biosocial View*, p. 67.
[10] C. J. Lumsden and E. O. Wilson, *Promethean Fire*, p. 176.
[11] Ibid., p. 133.
[12] M. E. Spiro, *Oedipus in the Trobriands*, p. 162.

existed in conditions comparable to those of modern open-country primates such as the gelada baboon. Geladas lack genetically-determined incest-avoidance mechanisms because structural characteristics of their society mean that young males are excluded from their father's harem groups when they become sexually mature. Such extrusion ensures that when such males as do mate acquire harems of their own the females in question are quite likely not to be their mothers and sisters.

As a possible development of a similar kind of adaptation in the past, modern human beings may well not have any deep-seated sexual aversion to near kin. Rather the contrary, because it seems probable that, thanks to the opportunities offered by the switch to a hunting economy, children may have begun to deploy sexual cues, both as a means of parental-seduction-in-the-interests-of-greater-investment but also, in the case of some males at least, as a means of persuading their mothers of their potentially superior Darwinian fitness as evidenced by sexual precocity and aggressiveness. As social evolution pushed parental counter-ploys – the repression of incestuous libido in particular and infantile, polymorphous sexuality in general – back from adolescent initiation into earlier and earlier periods of childhood, the developing personality of the child had increasingly to internalize the complex cultural prohibitions and ideals which corresponded to the ambient level of cultural evolution. Among these were the ubiquitous incest-taboos, first imposed only at adolescent initiation but, since at least the Neolithic, increasingly internalized in the pre-adolescent personality structure.

In short, what we have is a dynamic theory, one which takes biological determinants seriously, but which also does justice to the fact that those biological determinants only influence elaborated behaviour via a complex interaction with the environment, an important part of which is the correspondingly dynamic behaviour of others.

The mistake made by the crude biological determinist theory of incest-avoidance is to assume that, just because inbreeding is biologically deleterious and avoided in some other species by heritable, deterministic mechanisms of a relatively simple kind, the same must apply to human beings. A moment's reflection suffices to show that, even though inbreeding may be genetically undesirable, it does not necessarily have to have crude or automatic genetic determinants to prevent it. Any heritable mechanism or combination of mechanisms such as those proposed here would do as long as the result – a tendency to avoid inbreeding – was achieved.

By contrast to crude biological or cultural determinism – the only two types of explanation widely accepted up to now – the approach offered here will go some way to meet the three requirements listed above for a successful theory of the gene–behaviour interface. First, the theory self-evidently bases itself, both on the real existence of ultimate genetic determinants of behaviour, and on sound biological principles. Secondly, the theory does do justice to the complexity of actual human behaviour, mainly because, unlike the crude determinisms, it is dynamic and genuinely explains the interaction of individual motivations with the environment. Finally, the theory does solve the linkage problem, because by use of dynamic psychological processes, ultimately determined by inheritance but interacting with the environment and heavily shaped by it, it can show how basic biological functions (such as kin altruism) are carried out by specific psychological adaptations (such as identification) but can also account for apparent counter-trends and reactions (such as adolescent differentiation).

Outline of a third psychoanalytic topography

In bringing about such a synthesis of Freud and Darwin to provide the dynamic, psychological solution to the explanation of the gene–behaviour interface it will probably be necessary to propose changes to what has been called the second psychoanalytic topography. Now it may be necessary to modify the id–ego–superego schema somewhat to make it consistent with the new, sound biological foundation which we can provide for psychoanalytic theory.

In Freud's original schema the id is regarded as a chaotic, unstructured Inferno of biological drives and their dynamically repressed derivatives. Our new view leads us to see the id, by contrast, as highly structured by genetic factors which lay down the basic behavioural and psychological tendencies of human beings – such things as the propensity to form identifications and projections, to carry out repression, to regress, and so on. However, it also suggests that we should include in this unconscious, genetically-determined agency of the personality the fundamental basis of mechanisms which were previously assigned to the ego (or even superego), such as a tendency to induce feelings of guilt, and, above all, the fundamental mechanism producing repression and, thereby, the topography of consciousness. Furthermore, our new insights enable us to explain the exact adaptive significance of these genetically-determined elements: namely, the maximization of inclusive fitness.

In order to differentiate this new view of the id from the original one, but to maintain as far as possible the sense of similarity and continuity, we might rename it the system of *Inclusive-fitness-maximizing Demands* (or, alternatively, but less specifically, the *Instinctual Domain*), and represent both terms by the acronym 'ID'.

In what may perhaps eventually come to be regarded as a third topography, this ID might be seen, in accordance with the discussion above, as the genetically-determined substrate of the psyche, and its associated instinctual drives and structures as the means by which human beings are dynamically motivated to maximize their inclusive fitness – in other words, to serve the interests of their genes.

To use another metaphor, one might see it as the equivalent within the psychic constitution of the legislature in the government of a republic or constitutional monarchy. As such, it would lay down the laws which the executive agency must put into practice. The laws enacted there would be those representing the interests of the ultimate authority of the psychic government – the electorate of the genes.

In so far as this new ID is both genetically-determined and serves the ultimate interests of the genes, it can be thought of as a read-only memory in that its basic contents, like the contents of the genetic code itself, are laid down by evolution and not modified directly by the organism. This immediately explains the compulsive nature of dynamic repression, since anything rendered unconscious by repression is treated as part of the ID system and changes its status from the read/write registration which it had in consciousness to the read-only one existing in the ID. However, we also see that not all repressions need be pathological or even contrary to the self-interest of the individual because many repressions – such as those serving the interests of inclusive-fitness-maximization – in fact promote the interests of the individual despite rendering whole regions of consciousness inaccessible (as when individuals lie to themselves all the better to deceive others). The libido theory emerges naturally from this view, just as it does from Freud's original schema (although it is possible that it may require some extensive reformulation in future in the light of our rapidly increasing knowledge of the sociobiology of sexual behaviour).

If we are prepared to redefine Freud's id, then we might also think about reformulating our ideas about his 'ego', the psychological Purgatorio caught uncomfortably between the abysmal depths of the id and the outside world. This might be seen as the *Executive and Governing Organization*, 'EGO' for short, and conceived, analogously with the original meaning of 'ego', as an organization of the psyche ultimately charged with the execution of tactics which serve the grand strategy of the ID – the maximization of inclusive fitness. As such, it would exist as a natural complement to, and executive agency of, the inclusive-fitness-maximizing system whose demands upon it would create a dynamic tension whereby, with regard to sense data and the contingencies of external reality, the Executive and Governing Organization would be impelled to satisfy instinctual demands ultimately programmed to maximize fitness. Reverting to my earlier constitutional analogy, it would comprise the executive arm of the government of the mind and would be obliged to act in accordance with the laws laid down by the ID and would be expected to be always ultimately answerable to the latter.

One welcome consequence of this innovation might be the final break between the concept of the EGO as an agency and the 'I' as a personification of one's psyche. In the new view, the Executive and Governing Organization of the personality is much less likely to be mistaken for this subjective and tendentious self-concept. The latter might perhaps best be termed the *Persona*, and seen as a purely subjective image of the self, not necessarily coincident with objective psychological realities, and merely that part of the self-referential aspects of the preconscious field illuminated by consciousness (and therefore, by implication, serving the same tendentious, misinformative functions as many other aspects of consciousness).

In general, the new view of the EGO would see it as less autonomous and more governed by biological adaptations than the previous one which tended to see it in purely individual, ontogenetic terms. Now the EGO would emerge with a natural history, rather than merely an individual one, and would be considered more closely related to the ID, now that the latter's detailed structure is becoming clear, being seen ultimately as the executive agency to which the inclusive-fitness-maximizing demands of the genes were addressed.

Finally, Freud's 'superego', the Paradiso of religious, cultural and realistic values internalized by identification with parental figures, might be seen in the new view as a *Supernumerary Executive and Governing Organization*, or Super-EGO, for short. This would highlight its role as borrowed by identification from others and its remarkable ability to take over functions of command and control from the EGO in exceptional situations, such as powerful identifications which underlie hypnotic, religious or group-induced states of depersonalization. It would also be apt in suggesting the important possibilities for *externalization* – that is, the likelihood that external executive or governing organizations might usurp its functions (as where, thanks to induced altruism, agencies of social control take over important functions of the SuperEGO[13]). In terms of the constitutional metaphor, the SuperEGO would correspond to the supreme court of a republic or the King or Queen in a constitutional monarchy. It would be the representative of tradition and precedent and would function as the final court of appeal for the executive agency in cases where the ID could not legislate. It would be the symbolic repository of the cultural values of the personality, could override the legislature in certain circumstances and censor the executive (giving rise to the observed conflicts, both in its relations with the ID and with the EGO).

Summarizing the argument, we might say that, according to the dynamic, psychological solution to the problem of the gene–behaviour interface in human beings, genes relate to behaviour in the following way. They constitute, in psychological terms, a system of Inclusive-fitness-maximizing Demands, a wholly unconscious region in which various instinctual drives and dynamic psychological processes arise. Among the most important of these are identification and narcissistic projection which mediate kin altruism; differentiation and aggressive projection which are implicated in induced altruism; repression which is important in relation to reciprocal altruism but is also much more generally significant in determining mental topography; regression, reaction-formation and many other mechanisms all of which, it is assumed, evolved ultimately to serve the maximization of the inclusive fitness of their possessors.

[13] For a fuller discussion see C. Badcock, *Madness and Modernity*, chapters 5 and 6.

Because of the importance of sense-data in carrying out the grand, fitness-maximizing strategy of the ID, a part of it, an Executive and Governing Organization, acquires the principal function of command and control of voluntary movement. This EGO receives sense-data about the world outside and subjective innervations from its ID and its physical body on the basis of which instinctual demands influence it to act in a way which is presumed to be ultimately fitness-maximizing (Freud's Pleasure Principle).

However, in order to function effectively in a complex, cultural world, the EGO – especially in the young child – needs Supernumerary EGOs – especially those of the parents – first as outside helpers, and then, thanks to identification and internalization, as an inner, differentiated part of the EGO system containing cultural, religious and other values useful to the EGO in fulfilling the demands of the ID and in meeting the exigencies of reality. This SuperEGO is the true localization of culture within the individual and is in dynamic interaction with the ultimate biological determinants of the ID. Taken together, as an interacting system, the ID-EGO-SuperEGO mediates between the genes and behaviour and explains their relationship in human beings.

Finally, the internalization of the SuperEGO explains how cultural and environmental factors come to play the part which they do in human psychology. Unlike cultural-determinist theories which see these environmental factors as dominant in constituting psychology, the theory proposed here sees the EGO as dynamically responding to its environment on the basis of demands placed on it by an unconscious, repressed system of inclusive-fitness-maximizing drives. The theory sees this ID as unconscious because of the adaptive value in hiding self-seeking, fitness-maximizing demands behind a mask of apparent altruism and cooperativeness in a species in which social cooperation via reciprocal altruism is especially important. It also sees it as necessarily unconscious because of the need to maintain the compulsive nature of certain adaptations, such as the narcissistic identifications underlying the manifestation of kin altruism in our species.

One notable strength of this approach is that it can deal rather better than any kind of simple determinism with the full complexity and perversity of human behaviour and social arrangements. An example reverting to my earlier discussion of incest might be found in instances where the sibling incest-taboo has been temporarily suspended.

Hopkins has demonstrated that for a period of some 200 years brother–sister incest in Ptolemaic Egypt was not only condoned and openly celebrated, but that

> In the usable census returns, brother–sister marriages account for between 15 and 21 per cent of all ongoing marriages ($N = 113$). Crude demographic calculation suggests that in the conditions of high mortality prevalent in Roman Egypt, only about 40 per cent of all families had both a son *and* a daughter or both sons *and* daughters surviving to marriage-able age. This means that one-third, and perhaps more, of all brothers with marriageable sisters married inside the family in preference to marrying a woman from outside the family.[14]

Far from finding a 'biopsychical mechanism' which makes sibling incest-avoidance 'natural in the full biological sense', Hopkins comes to the 'tentative conclusion that Egyptian brothers and sisters married each other because they themselves wanted to.'[15] Short of suggesting that the gene for preventing sibling incest got temporarily lost or that – contrary to the facts – such incestuous siblings were not raised in close domestic intimacy, the biological-determinist theory of incest-avoidance must have great difficulty in explaining this finding.

Not so the theory advanced here. Since the SuperEGO is a supernumerary, acquired department of the EGO its functions can be, and indeed sometimes are, carried on by other executive and governing organizations, such as state agencies

---

[14] K. Hopkins, 'Brother–Sister Marriage in Roman Egypt', *Comparative Studies in Society and History*, 22, 1980, p. 304.
[15] Ibid., p. 353.

of social control. As long as some external or internal agency of social control exists to ensure that the latent war of all men against all other men for the control of all the women does not break out, civilized human society can continue. In developed centralized bureaucratic states like Roman Egypt the social structure was in no very important way threatened by sibling incest, indeed, as Hopkins suggests, important positive interests of the family may have been served by it. However, such could not have been the case in primal hunter-gatherer societies. In societies such as these, where external agencies enforcing the induced altruism of the state rather than derivations of the kin altruism of the family had not evolved, no such relaxation of one of the basic incest-taboos could have occurred for any significant period of time. There, as Roheim showed in his study of Australian aborigines, incest was 'the greatest of all crimes against the social order' whose ultimate punishment was usually death.[16]

In other words, what can be achieved by internalized restraint based on primal kin identification can also be achieved by external means drawing on the bureaucratization of induced altruism in states where governmental institutions have taken over some of the roles of the individual Super-EGO. Although complete abolition of all incest-taboos in such circumstances would be unlikely, some relaxation seems conceivable and it can hardly be accidental that in the modern world proposals to legalize sibling incest were first heard in Sweden, the epitome of modern bureaucratic welfare states.

Insight and induced altruism

The ability to explain such apparently puzzling counter-examples as this one must be one of the main virtues of the dynamic theory of human motivation and the revised

[16] G. Roheim, 'The Primal Horde and Incest in Central Australia', *Journal of Criminal Psychopathology*, 3, 1942, p. 459.

psychoanalytic topography suggested here. However, the merits of the theory are hardly likely to be the only factor which determines its acceptance or rejection, as the theory itself would predict.

On the contrary, one might expect it to encounter resistance over its most important insights: those relating to deceit in general and to the theory of induced altruism in particular. This is because deceit, parasitism, manipulation, exploitation and even crude predation will usually pay an organism, if it can get away with it. It follows that scientific theories which make it harder for human beings to get away with it will not be welcome to the erstwhile instigators of induced altruism, no matter what their technique may be. Furthermore, the outlook is even more dismal for the theory because the most effective deceivers will be the self-deceivers who genuinely do not know that they are deceiving themselves even though the practical consequence of their self-deception is to improve their scope for exploiting others. Admittedly, sometimes self-deception may be a defence against being exploited by others, as when someone rationalizes a piece of self-interest in altruistic terms in order not to be induced to confer some benefit on another. In general though, self-deception, merely because of the implicit cost in reducing the self-awareness of the subject and thereby proportionately increasing their ignorance of reality, is a dangerous tactic only justifiable by its ultimate benefit in securing sacrifices to the subject's advantage by others. If the sacrifices cannot be secured the cost may outweigh the benefit until, as Trivers notes, 'self-deception induces a range of impaired learning that may have costs far removed from the initial acts generating the impulse towards self-deception.'[17]

Yet the outlook for such a theory is not completely bleak, any more than the sociobiological theory of human consciousness is all on the side of emphasizing self-deception at the expense of self-awareness.

[17] R. Trivers, 'Sociobiology and Politics', in E. White (ed.), *Sociobiology and Human Politics*, p. 26.

If we accept that self-deception pays, we must also accept that evolution will probably reward successful defence against the worst consequences of such a technique when deployed by others. For instance, as Trivers also notes, 'humans seem to make distinctions about altruism partly on the basis of motive, a tendency that is consistent with the hypothesis that such discrimination is relevant to protecting oneself from cheaters.'[18] Such a concern with motive may well prejudice people against a theory like the one being presented here which appears to ignore it altogether in its apparently stubborn and wrong-headed emphasis on the objective consequences of altruistic acts, rather than their subjective intentions. Yet a deeper understanding of the points I am making immediately leads to new insights into human motivation: we see that, precisely because motive is, scientifically speaking, a useless concept in animal behaviour, we are able to develop a general theory of altruism which, whilst not accepting motives as defining altruistic acts in any way, nevertheless soon enables us to understand why motives matter in the practice of human altruism and why they may be used both to further self-deception, as well as to reveal it.

Indeed, we soon see that the best modern insights into human motives, those provided by psychoanalysis, beautifully complement the general biological theory and bear out its principal theorem: nature abhors altruism in the pure sense. As we have seen, if culture adores it, and religion, philosophy and all that is apparently best in human life agrees, then it is really only because it is so abhorrent that it can safely be prescribed for others – their induced altruistic masochism corresponds to my projected but virtuously-disguised sadism (Nietzsche's Principle). Our new insight into the motive for cultural idealism about altruism is clearly a major weapon against induced altruism because anyone who fully understands the principle will think twice before accepting any recommendation to act altruistically at its face value

[18] Ibid., p. 21.

and will certainly become somewhat critical about general admonitions to altruism, particularly on the part of those who stand to gain at the altruist's expense.

Yet, quite apart from general principles, it is likely that human psychology has not only evolved to detect cheating but that it has also evolved one of its most justly-prized attributes as an adaptation against the specific consequence of the deceptions practised by others: I mean our capacity for true insight.

This is because deception will usually be deployed, both in oneself and against others, as a means of inducing altruistic sacrifices in others. The consequence of induced altruism is that one is preyed upon, parasitized, manipulated, exploited and generally manoeuvred into a self-sacrifice which one would not have wanted to make. Self-awareness is an obvious defence against such manipulations because if I can become aware of what I am doing – particularly in relation to my real self-interest – then I may be able to prevent it, get out of it, or modify its worst effects. Knowing where I am, what is happening to me and what the consequences of my actions are likely to be is not merely a means of simple existence, but becomes crucially significant in circumstances in which things are happening to me which I would not wish, where I am not where I think I am and where the outcome of my actions may be other than in my best interests.

In the context of competitive induced altruism, even as it must have existed within primal societies, it is not difficult to see how the EGO may have evolved, not merely to become conscious of what could be avowed and to become un-conscious of what could not, but also to obtain reliable self-perceptions regarding what it might be induced to be conscious of, what it had been induced to do and what the consequences of its decisions might be. In particular, such insight might be needed as a defence against hostile projec-tions which impute undesirable things to oneself actually present in the imputer. By having reliable information about one's true motives one might be better able to counter slanderous accusations by others and deploy what is usually a highly effective, if slow-acting counter to lies – namely, the truth.

Furthermore, conscious access to aspects of one's mental processing seems to connote a read/write ability by contrast to the read-only registration in the unconscious. Whilst the compulsive, read-only character of certain motives may be desirable (such as the introjection of the aggression of pastoralists which I mentioned earlier), in other circumstances it might clearly not promote one's inclusive fitness to act compulsively. Nowhere would this be more true than in cases where one's compulsive action was in the interests of another to whom one was not related and which had been brought about by manipulation or deceit. In these circumstances it would pay the EGO to be able to have access to the motives in question and review their status, desirability and general utility to itself and its ID, perhaps with a view to changing or modifying them. In this way conscious self-reference would mean not merely insight, but also initiative, and would be all the more effective the more accurate and reliable were the insights in question.

In short, if lies might be effective defences against truth, then truth might in some circumstances be an equally effective defence against lies; and if the truth in question were the truth about oneself, then it would nowhere be more valuable than in countering lies which others might use against oneself. If such true insights could also allow one to modify one's behaviour in accordance with them one might have the evolutionary basis not merely for self-deception, but also for its opposite – true insight.

Much the same applies to social theory. Here, too, truth can be made to pay if it is an effective antidote to lies and if true insights into reality can be deployed as a defence against tendentious ones whose consequence is to damage one's own interests. Furthermore, the fact of ever-increasing social differentiation will mean that social and psychological theories which serve the interests of some in inducing altruistic sacrifice in others will not serve the interests of the others whose sacrifice is being induced. They will look around for alternative interpretations of what is going on and will be attracted by theories which reveal the state of affairs from their point of view. As we saw earlier, one of the great virtues of the theory of induced altruism is that it depicts predation, parasitism, exploitation, manipulation and deceit from the point of view of the preyed-upon, parasitized, exploited, manipulated and deceived parties. It is emphatically in their interests to have some insight into what is going on just as it is equally emphatically in the interests of the instigators of their altruism to maintain the customary deceptions which hide and justify their exploitation.

Of course, the whole issue becomes unbearably complicated and messy when one notices that in modern, bureaucratized and highly differentiated societies everyone is someone else's other, and every other, someone else's one. In other words, someone who may be a victim of induced altruism in one context may be an instigator and beneficiary in some other respect. Indeed, it might pay the more powerfully placed and proficient exploiters of the system to try to bring this about because, by implicating everyone in elaborate ties of mutual exploitation, deceit and manipulation, it may be possible to see that no one has any real incentive to break out of the game as a whole, even though, inevitably, some will benefit much more than others and the vast majority will probably find that the costs of the system greatly outweigh its benefits, making it a liability to everyone. Then indeed the collective interest may seem to be in realizing the truth about what is going on but the fact that large group interests and those of the individuals who make them up seldom if ever agree means that this is not usually the case.

However, the interests of some will always be best served by opposing those of others, and so it seems that, even though it is naïve to assume that it will be in everyone's interests to change a system which penalizes the majority, it is nevertheless probably true that it will usually be in someone's interests to advocate what, in reality, may well be in the best interests of all.

Reaction, revolution and reciprocity

In a well-known book,[19] Robert Axelrod published the results and analysis of a tournament he held for computer programs designed to play reiterated Prisoner's Dilemma. The reiterated version of the game has players making choices to cooperate or defect in exactly the way outlined earlier, but with knowledge of the outcome of the previous moves in the game. Numerical values attached to the various payoffs for cooperation and defection produced scores which indicated the relative success of the various programs entered in the tournament. Programs differed only in their strategy or *decision rule*: the means they used to decide whether to cooperate or defect in the circumstances of their opponent's past performance and their own.

Axelrod shows that, as long as the payoff values do not decline too quickly with time, there is no best strategy independent of the strategy of the other player.[20] This is easily shown. Imagine that the opposing program uses the strategy called ALL D, one in which it defects on every move. Clearly, one can do no better than defect every time as well, since to cooperate will win the maximum payoff for ALL D and the minimum for oneself. However, playing ALL D against itself will not win the highest score possible since the payoff for mutual defection is less than that for

---

[19] R. Axelrod, *The Evolution of Cooperation.*

[20] Ibid., p. 15. Here I ignore the more technical mathematical aspects of reiterated Prisoner's Dilemma which readers can find fully explained in Axelrod's book.

successful defection or reciprocal cooperation.[21] The highest possible score, by contrast, could be obtained by playing ALL D against a program which always cooperates, what we may perhaps call SUCKER. Since there is the greatest quantitive disparity between the payoff for successful defection and unsuccessful cooperation in Prisoner's Dilemma, SUCKER is certainly the worst possible strategy (which is why, needless to say, no one actually entered this program in the tournament). Furthermore, we will recall that we have already noted the the drawbacks of unconditional cooperation when I pointed out that it was the Prisoner's Dilemma equivalent of Nietzsche's Principle.[22]

As far as a best strategy is concerned, one might think that the winning program would have to be very complex because very devious. Presumably it would be one which would tempt its opponent into unguarded cooperations and then defect when least expected and when least vulnerable to retaliation, perhaps towards the end of the game. Such programs did compete in the tournament (one of the more successful ones was aptly named TRANQUILIZER), but the winner was actually the shortest and least complex of all. Called TIT FOR TAT, its decision rule was extremely simple and ran as follows: cooperate on the first move and thereafter do whatever your opponent did on the previous move.

TIT FOR TAT seems to have been so successful mainly because of its immediate and discriminating *reciprocity*. For instance, if playing against ALL D, it will lose the first game by cooperating, but will do no worse than its opponent thereafter. However, if it encounters an opponent ready to cooperate it will reciprocate and score rather better than in the previous case. Not only is it forgiving and unwilling to be the first to defect (*nice* in the technical jargon), it is also

---

[21] It will be recalled that if T is the payoff for successful defection, R that for successfully cooperating, P that for mutual defection and S the sucker's payoff (unreciprocated cooperation) we have the relation $T > R > P > S$ and we assume that $R > (T + S)/2$. After Axelrod, Ibid.

[22] See above pp. 143–4.

unexploitative, as is shown by considering how it treats SUCKER, the strategy of unconditional cooperation. Obviously, both strategies will begin by cooperating on the first move and will continue to do so for the rest of the game, both winning the payoff for reciprocity (and resulting in SUCKER doing substantially better against TIT FOR TAT than ALL D did!). However, perhaps the most surprising thing about its performance when pitted against less accommodating programs is that

> TIT FOR TAT . . . never received more points in any game than the other player! Indeed, it can't possibly score more than the other player in a game because it always lets the other player defect first, and it will never defect more times than the other player does. It won, not by doing better than any other player, but by eliciting cooperation from the other player. In this way TIT FOR TAT does well by promoting the mutual interest rather than by exploiting the other's weakness. A moral person couldn't do much better.[23]

If cooperation corresponds to reciprocal altruism in single-interaction Prisoner's Dilemma, TIT FOR TAT corresponds to it in the reiterated version; while ALL D in the reiterated version corresponds to defection in the individual game. It is a strategy of pure, predatory induced altruism. Despite this, the fact that TIT FOR TAT won the tournament strongly argues for its robustness and survivability, something underlined by an evolutionary evaluation of the competing programs which weighted their survival against past success over thousands of 'generations' and again confirmed TIT FOR TAT as the winner.[24]

Although these findings originate from a purely abstract, mathematical model of social interactions they have numerous clear parallels with reality as Axelrod and Hamilton show. Situations as diverse as the Live-and-Let-Live conventions which evolved in trench warfare in World War I to

---

[23] R. Axelrod, *The Evolution of Cooperation*, p. 137.
[24] See *ibid.*, pp. 48–54.

interactions of cancer genes and their hosts have been persuasively shown to illustrate the basic principles of Prisoner's Dilemma. It does not seem unreasonable to suppose that, given the inevitable limitations of mathematical modelling of complex real-life situations, Prisoner's Dilemma and in particular the surprising success of TIT FOR TAT teach important lessons for basic social theory. As I now hope to be able to suggest, the robustness, reliability and realism of TIT FOR TAT as demonstrated by Axelrod may also apply to the more complex embodiments of the principle of reciprocity found in the modern world.

The general theory of altruism, when applied to human societies, suggests that the three fundamental forms of altruism correspond to three fundamental forms of social structure, depending upon which type of altruism is uppermost in the society in question. Traditional societies, as I suggested earlier, are evidently founded on the expansion of kin altruism through identification with pseudo-kin groups such as the tribe, nation or race. Their leaders are usually father- or mother-figures, their territory also often quasi-parental in the cultural symbolism. These societies idealize what Emile Durkheim called 'mechanical solidarity', a form of altruistic commitment to the group based on identification, often real enough in the local community but projected and fantasized for the larger group, if it exists. Increasingly in the modern world, where population expansion and economic growth have greatly undermined traditional, small-scale society, such social structures look, and often are, reactionary in the sense that they strive, sometimes quite openly, to restore a lost and probably irretrievable stage of social evolution.

If reaction aims to restore kin altruism as the basis of the social structure, then revolution usually connotes induced altruism and bureaucratization. Revolutionary societies attempt to destroy previous social and economic structures in order to create new ones which are always bureaucratic and usually tyrannical thanks to the social consequences of induced altruism and its inherently predatory nature. In such societies social solidarity is supposed to come about naturally but, because ideal altruism is not a part of human behaviour and so cannot be exploited in practice to any very great extent, such societies either fall back on patriotic or ethnic identification as the basis for social solidarity or enforce it by coercion, or try to do both.

For instance, according to Marx's social theory, individuals will become naturally altruistic and cooperative once they are no longer exploited by private property thanks to socialization of the means of production. In terms of Prisoner's Dilemma this amounts to an expectation that individuals will not be tempted to exploit a strategy of unconditional cooperation (SUCKER). However, there is not the slightest rational reason for believing that this is so, and overwhelming grounds for thinking the contrary. Indeed, if one reflects on the sad fact of vandalism and its link with public goods one can see that the exact opposite seems to be true: public goods which promote the welfare of some more than others are likely to be vandalized by the others in order to reduce the advantage they confer on some.

(This apparently idealistic belief in the virtues of unconditional cooperation takes on a quite different complexion when one recalls that revolution amounts to unconditional defection analogous to ALL D in reiterated Prisoner's Dilemma. In politics one often gets the feeling that Marxist idealism about human altruism actually means expecting others to cooperate unconditionally with the radical defection of the revolutionaries. In short, it looks like an ideological justification for getting others to play SUCKER – with predictable results for the others wherever such revolutions have succeeded.)

Lacking a genuine psychological mechanism specific to the form of altruism in question, societies based on induced altruism exploit deception to an unprecedented degree (for instance, in trying to persuade the majority that things are done in its interest) and fall back on the one psychological tendency which can be exploited – the projection of aggression against outsiders. This tends to make such societies not merely bureaucratized and heavily internally-policed but also paranoid in their foreign relations and militaristic to a high degree. Furthermore, it throws some not entirely creditable light on the fascination which many sociologists seem to have for induced altruism and its social consequences and explains why the official ideologies of such societies are social rather than traditional theologies.

Of course, such ideal types are not in practice exclusive. The Third Reich represents a particularly obnoxious mixture both of the kin altruistic elements (which made it *National* Socialism), and induced altruism (which made it National *Socialism*) and resulted in particularly virulent paranoid projections of aggression against the Jews and other despised ethnic minorities. Today the cult of Lenin as the national father of the socialist revolution in the USSR reflects a similar mixing of types.

Finally, a society can base itself on reciprocal altruism and organize its social solidarity through free exchange (what Durkheim called 'organic solidarity'). By contrast to the two former types, such societies will be notably free and open because lacking either the central organization inseparable from bureaucratically-induced altruism or the traditional authority represented by the rulers of kin-based societies. This is because, as Axelrod's mathematical modelling of interaction suggests, reiterated reciprocity (TIT FOR TAT) can cause cooperation to emerge and be sustained in a world of egoists without central control and with only their self-interest as a motive (consider the astonishing cooperation between ostensible enemies in World War I described in his book). In the words of Adam Smith:

> It is not from the benevolence of the butcher, the brewer, or the baker that we expect our dinner, but from their regard for their own self-interest. We address ourselves, not to their

humanity but to their self-love, and never talk to them of our own necessities but of their advantages.[25]

Had we, in Smith's words, 'addressed ourselves to their humanity' we should quite clearly have been soliciting one of the two other kinds of altruism, and would have tried to exploit their benevolence either out of some appeal to moral obligation (induced altruism) or by means of their empathic identification with our dinnerless state (the psychological basis of kin altruism). Smith describes reciprocal altruism perfectly when he comments that

> man has almost constant occasion for the help of his brethren, and it is in vain for him to expect it from their benevolence only. He will be more likely to prevail if he can interest their self-love in his favour, and show them that it is for their own advantage to do for him what he requires of them. Whoever offers to another a bargain of any kind, proposes to do this. Give me that which I want, and you shall have this which you want, is the meaning of every such offer.[26]

As F. A. Hayek has suggested, such a social structure might be best described as a *catallaxy*[27] and, in terms of the general theory of altruism, might be defined as one based on generalized, indirect and multiparity reciprocal altruism (or, in terms of Prisoner's Dilemma, one based on the winning strategy of TIT FOR TAT). Such, of course, is the natural subject-matter of economics, at least of the classical, liberal kind.

If traditional societies reflect the basis of their structure in being essentially the products of identification and ethnic cohesiveness and if bureaucratic ones reflect a corresponding reality in being dominated by legalistic coercion, then catal-laxies are characterized by being based on individual self-interest, reciprocity and free exchange. Such societies will

[25] A. Smith, *The Wealth of Nations*, p. 119.
[26] Ibid., p. 118.
[27] F. A. Hayek, *Law, Legislation and Liberty*, vol. II, pp. 108–9.

tend to lack the ethnic or traditional cohesiveness of those based on kin identification and the obvious orderliness of those based on bureaucratic regimentation, but they will have strengths of their own, not the least of which will be their ability to innovate, adapt and respond to changing conditions. This is notoriously absent in traditional societies, which, by definition, find their strength in their resistance to change and their foundation in the past and in tradition. It is also notably absent in bureaucratic ones where the appearance of bureaucratic competence in making altruistic decisions – that is, those supposed to be in the best interests of everybody – is often far from the reality and always founded on the fallacy of holistic interests (which, as we saw earlier, tendentiously claims that individual and group interests are identical).

In the catallaxy, by contrast, individuals are presumed to be most competent in judging what is in their own interests and, in a manner typical of reciprocal altruism, individual self-interest is harnessed to that of other individuals via free exchange. This is in sharp contrast to traditional societies, where inherited or religious privilege obtrudes to make some individuals judged more competent in making decisions for others than the others themselves; and much the same comes about in bureaucratic societies where alleged bureaucratic 'expertise' makes bureaucrats qualified to decide what is in the best interests of those whom they administer. The practical consequence is that, in societies based on free exchange, individuals acquire a degree of dignity, freedom, equality and independence seldom if ever found in anything but the elites in other societies, and often not even there to anything like the same extent.

Yet, of course, pure catallaxies are as unlikely to exist in reality as either of the two previous forms, and perhaps even less likely. This is because certain aspects of social life will maintain other altruistic foundations for perfectly natural reasons. Family relationships are still most likely to function on the basis of identification and kin altruism, just as certain inescapably legalistic aspects of life like the maintenance of law and order are likely to manifest induced altruism to a considerable extent. Furthermore, in a society based on free exchange, deceit, cheating and therefore induced rather than reciprocal altruism is to be expected for reasons already explained. Free-riding and defection will always pay if individuals can get away with it and, by definition, free-riding and defection means inducing unreciprocated altruistic sacrifice in others.

Such attempts to subvert the basic reciprocity on which a free-exchange society depends will take many forms apart from obvious dishonesty, cheating and corruption in face-to-face interactions. Compared with the more subtle deceits which can be all too easily practised in complex societies with high degrees of differentiation, the deceptions involved in simple fraud seem almost honest and straightforward. Robbery, burglary or theft, even if needing sophisticated computer skills or complex technical apparatus, seem simple and direct compared to the subtle deceits involved in manipulating public expenditure in favour of pressure-groups, business interests or whatever. At least the thief knows he is thieving; very often the most effective manipulators of modern societies steal shamelessly, convinced that they are public benefactors.

Yet so insidious and inevitable is the process whereby induced altruism comes to supplant genuine reciprocity that the economist Mancur Olson (to whom we were indebted earlier for our insights into the holistic fallacy and the free-rider theorem) has recently advanced a theory of economic growth and decline based, among others, on the following general principles:

> Stable societies with unchanged boundaries tend to accumulate more collusions and organizations for collective action over time.[28]

[28] M. Olson, *The Rise and Decline of Nations*, p. 74. All the following quotations are from the same source.

G

In other words, left to itself a society will find that time alone allows for pluralities such as pressure-groups and special interests to organize themselves to counter purely individualistic and reciprocal action. In terms of the general theory of altruism suggested here this will reduce genuine reciprocal altruism and substitute predatory, induced altruism with less than beneficial results:

> On balance, special-interest organizations and collusions reduce efficiency and aggregate income in the societies in which they operate and make political life more divisive.

What he terms 'distributional coalitions' attempt to substitute induced or kin-based principles of altruism for individualistic reciprocity and

> make decisions more slowly than the individuals and firms of which they are composed, tend to have crowded agendas and bargaining tables, and fix prices rather than quantities . . . Distributional coalitions slow down a society's capacity to adopt new technologies and to reallocate resources in response to changing conditions, and thereby reduce the rate of economic growth . . . The accumulation of distributional coalitions increases the complexity of regulation, the role of government, and the complexity of understandings, and changes the direction of social evolution.

In short, they substitute induced or kin altruism for reciprocal altruism in economic matters and drive a society towards the bureaucratic or traditional rather than the catallactic type.

This, of course, will always be in the interests of some, but never in the interests of all, and usually distinctly not in the interests of others. Furthermore, it will not be in the interests of the whole society's adaptation to future changes in its socio-economic environment. What Olson accurately calls distributional coalitions will succeed in formalizing constraints on free exchange between individuals in such a way that the market mechanism will function less efficiently in communicating between producers, consumers, and buyers and sellers of all kinds.

Contrary to the ideological statements disseminated by apologists for reaction or revolution – that is, in our terms, generalized kin or induced altruism – and contrary also to some misinformed apologists for reciprocal altruism and the free market, the function of free-market exchanges is not a moral one, aimed at rewarding virtue, hard work or skill, but is a purely communicative one. Rewards such as profits, pay and remunerations of all kinds are not economic substitutes for the just judgements of providence, a system for recognizing individual merit, or even evidence of grace in the eyes of a deity who believes in thrift and hard work. They act purely as signals, indicating where effort and the application of resources will be rewarded with success and where they will not.[29]

In terms of the theory being elaborated here, they act as generally reliable indicators in the complex communications which constitute reciprocal interactions. I say generally reliable indicators because, unlike verbal assertions or other purely arbitrary communications, the exchange of goods and services actually represents valuable resources and as such powerfully engages the self-interest of their owners. It costs little to say that one believes in some product, or that one supports some cause, much more to actually purchase it or pay up. Unlike the general, diffuse verbalizations or bureaucratic norms which underlie altruism of the induced kind, the specific self-interest involved in personal expenditure, whether of time, effort or money, can usually be relied upon to indicate much more genuinely the true intentions and motives of the actor in question. The great virtue of the catallaxy, as opposed to other forms of social structure, is that, in reducing the greater part of social interaction to market-mediated free exchanges, it obliges individuals to betray their real self-interests in literally putting their money where their mouth is and showing, by actually offering

[29] F. A. Hayek, *Law, Legislation and Liberty*, vol. II, p. 74.

something of value, that they are ready to reciprocate for whatever they want.

This is in direct contrast to the bureaucratic or traditional society where privilege or entitlement defined by convention or law will enable some individuals to demand some things from others for which they need make no return. Furthermore, in such societies mere assertion by traditionally- or bureaucratically-defined competent persons will suffice to indicate to others how they should act and dispose their resources. Since, thanks to the complexity, unpredictability and general fluidity of the reality of human interaction with others and with our environment, such allegedly competent traditional or bureaucratic authority-figures can seldom be right all of the time about the things they are supposed to adminster and control and can frequently be ludicrously wrong, traditional and bureaucratic societies experience low or negligible levels of innovation and often dangerously slow adaptation to change.

In part then, the superior adaptability, dynamism and capacity for all kinds of innovation found in free-exchange societies of the catallactic type derives from the greater reliability and realism of the information involved in their fundamental interactions. Because reciprocal altruism is founded on realistic self-interest which can only yield its best results if articulated via free exchange with the comparable self-interest of others, catallaxies promote levels of response to individual and social needs far superior to those of traditional or bureaucratic societies where the spontaneous initiative of free individuals is suppressed by the dead hand of traditionalism or bureaucratic interference.

As Axelrod's computer simulations showed, uncomplicated reciprocity (TIT FOR TAT) promotes higher final payoffs to both parties than mutual competition to defect. A corollary of this insight is that the final outcome is not a zero-sum game, that is, one in which more for one party means less for another: 'in a non-zero-sum world you do not have to do better than the other player in order to do well yourself.'[30] In the economic sphere, for instance, Marxism teaches that life indeed is a zero-sum game (labour value added to one party must be lost to another producing 'alienation' in the loser), yet the general increase in wealth and welfare of free-exchange societies as compared with Marxist ones strongly argues against this, and for the conclusion suggested by the success of TIT FOR TAT. Its success also highlights the crudities of Social Darwinism, which, substituting competitive individuals for competing classes,[31] also made the mistake of regarding economic activity as a zero-sum game equivalent to 'fitness'. It seems that, where reciprocity is given a chance, economic success can reward both sides of an exchange, so that the final gain to both exceeds the selfish rewards of defection by either. The refutation of both Marxism and Social Darwinism lies in the realization that cooperation, whether between individuals or classes, yields more to both parties than competition.

A striking and counter-intuitive example of the latter which suggests that this principle goes considerably further than conventional maxims about cooperation being preferable to confrontation is provided by what at first sight seems a prime case of the zero-sum game, taxation. Here, it would appear, more for the government means less for the taxpayer and vice versa. However that may be, the following quotation suggests that, even in this instance, cooperation can yield more to both parties than defection:

> The income tax does indeed 'soak the rich' – but that soaking does not yield much revenue to the government. It rather takes the form of inducing the rich to acquire costly tax shelters and rearrange their affairs in other ways that will minimize actual tax payments. There is a very large wedge

[30] Axelrod, *The Evolution of Cooperation*, p. 112.
[31] Marx, it should be recalled, wanted to dedicate *Das Kapital* to Darwin.

between the cost to the taxpayer and the revenue to the government. The magnitude of that wedge was illustrated by the reduction in 1981 of the top rate on so-called unearned income from 70 to 50 per cent. Despite ensuing recession, the taxes actually paid at rates of 50 per cent and above went up, *not down*, as a result.[32]

In other words, what happened was that defection by tax-avoidance on the part of higher earners was replaced by more cooperation with taxation once the government increased its own cooperation by lowering top rates. Here, astonishingly, both government taxation *and* personal income increased, despite recession. It seems that even where altruism has to be basically induced, as in income taxation, reciprocity can still yield superior returns to the soak-the-rich-socialism of Marx and his followers.

Societies based on kin or induced altruism never succeed in solving the problem of 'Who guards the guardians?' because their social systems require guardians who have a privileged and superior position, naturally putting them above control. In a catallaxy, however, there is a solution: lack of traditional or bureaucratic guardianship makes each free individual a guardian of their own interests – interests which, after all, only the individual is competent to judge. As Axelrod demonstrated, reciprocity can bring cooperation even into a world of self-interested egoists. But since committees and collectivities seldom possess the originality or the creativity of individuals, they function just as poorly as guardians of innovation and adaptation as they do of anything else except their own privileges. In the catallaxy, however, free exchange between self-interested parties results in economic and social transactions functioning with an information-carrying efficiency far surpassing that of either of the other two fundamental social types.

(To deny this individualism reveals the latent paternalism and elitism of traditional and bureaucratic attitudes: they

[32] M. and R. Friedman, *The Tyranny of the Status Quo*, p. 67 (Friedmans' emphasis).

have to pretend that individuals are not competent to judge their own best interests and, if put into practice as forms of government, rapidly produce the effects they claim are 'natural': a subservient, incompetent and disadvantaged mass under an arrogant leadership. Considerations such as these put the socialistic obsession with disadvantage of all kinds in a new and sinister light because, as the theory might suggest, altruistic concern for others' welfare need not only originate in identification. Exaggerated concern for others can just as easily reflect a desire to put oneself in a position of control over them as one based on identification with them and, if it stresses their incompetence to choose for themselves, naturally absolves one from the need for genuine reciprocal relations with them. This is probably the basis for the widespread and well-founded suspicion of professional altruists of all kinds.)

Not surprisingly, traditional societies based on kin altruism will prefer traditional social theories which stress identification. Since the latter is an unconscious dynamic psychological process it cannot, of course, be directly invoked, but the religious, nationalistic or ethnic myths which promote such identifications will be exploited to the full. Something like the punitive monotheism of the Nuer or Dinka might appear paradigmatic here because it encompasses both the strong focus for identification via the deity-as-shared-SuperEGO of the group, and the self-sacrificing masochism resulting from the introjection of aggressive drives. Religions of a comparable kind, along with their associated traditional social theory, law and custom can therefore be expected to be exploited – an expectation recently strongly borne out by experience.

Bureaucratic societies, by contrast, those ostensibly founded on revolution rather than reaction, can be expected to promote holistic social theories which stress the subservience of the individual to the group and its self-appointed leaders. Such theories will collectively fall under the heading 'Socialism' and will function as apologies and rationalizations for induced altruism as defined here. In practice they will be overwhelmingly bureaucratized and will find as one of their principal functions of social control the necessity to suppress social and scientific theories which appear to conflict with official doctrine, much as nuclear physics was proscribed in the Soviet Union until the advent of atomic weapons and Mendelian genetics was not fully accepted until 1981 (with catastrophic results for Soviet agriculture).[33]

Finally, free exchange societies based on reciprocal altruism will inevitably favour real as opposed to official science, and fact as opposed to traditional fantasy. This is because, as we saw just now, their social system functions on the basis of realism. Practical realism about motivation leads naturally to the Darwinian-Freudian foundations of our insights into social behaviour and on to the general theory of altruism outlined here. The individualism and reductionism of the Freudian-Darwinian view naturally complements the practical individualism of the catallaxy and the latter's rejection of central overall control nicely reflects the critique of holism implicit both in psychoanalysis and sociobiology. The essentially open, non-dogmatic and provisional nature of scientific knowledge exactly mirrors the free, controversial nature of the catallaxy where uncoerced exchange between free individuals stands as the basis both of the economy and of the media of communication, including those of science. (In traditional or bureaucratic societies, by contrast, we can expect to find psychoanalysis proscribed (as it is today in the USSR) and it does not require prophetic gifts to see that the same fate will befall the resurgence of authentic Darwinism in sociobiology.)

Such are, of course, only ideal types. In reality, many reactions will claim to be 'revolutions', and many revolutions turn out to be reactions. Most ostensibly free societies today are more bureaucratized than is generally realized, and one or two may well follow through this line of evolution to actual closure and complete bureaucratization. Some allegedly

---

[33] N. J. Marks, *Science and the Making of the Modern World*, p. 397.

archetypically open societies were in fact much closer to the catallactic ideal in the past than today, and – inevitably, given the realities of human nature – many ostensibly bureaucratized societies make provision for free exchange of some kinds and are always being undermined by unofficial reciprocity – the ubiquitous 'black markets'.

Nevertheless, if the three fundamental forms of altruism are indeed exhaustive it seems that they are likely increasingly to reveal themselves, not merely in behavioural and social terms, but in geopolitical ones as well when modern societies, faced with the dilemmas of adaptation to increasing population and competition for resources, have to choose between reaction, revolution or reciprocity. Both reaction and revolution will exert strong appeal but both will ultimately prove to be less adaptive than reciprocity because only the latter can sustain the level of economic growth, technological innovation and scientific progress which modern populations come increasingly to expect, whatever the fundamental basis of their social structure.

Psychoanalysis and the future of free societies

In its first, formative period psychoanalysis encountered personality structures in its patients which were largely traditional and centred on secure and often punitive SuperEGOs, themselves based on powerful identifications. Hysteria, the paradigmatic mental disorder of the day, also featured strong tendencies to identification and the early psychotherapeutic method of hypnotism was the ultimate in suggestive identification and narcissistic projection. Under hypnosis the psychotherapist became an actual supernumerary EGO of the patient so that patient and therapist formed a psychological group of two in which the leader – the hypnotist – achieved powers of suggestion and control over his subject only seen – and then very rarely – in larger groups under conditions of real mass hysteria.

As the mature psychoanalytic method of *analysis* rather than suggestion emerged, it came to seem counter-reactionary (in the sense of the word used here) in that analysis undid the compulsive nature of unconscious identifications by making them accessible to consciousness and putting the energies tied up in them at the disposal of the EGO. This undoing of repression suggested to many that psychoanalysis was a natural ally of social theories which sought to undo alleged social and political repressions (despite the fact that the psychoanalytic meaning of the term 'repression' is almost the exact opposite of that employed in political slogans). Consequently, psychoanalysis was interpreted as a revolutionary doctrine, and a large number of writers (whose one common denominator seems to have been that they were more devoted to revolution than psychoanalysis) sought to bring about a synthesis of analysis and socialism in general, and of Freud and Marx in particular. Certainly, during its second, mature phase psychoanalysis seems to have been implicitly allied in the minds of many, if not with Marxism, at least with the milder bureaucratic interventionism of the age of Keynes, which largely coincided with it.

Today this second phase of psychoanalysis may be closing; it is certainly true that many of the revolutionaries have long since despaired of enlisting Freud in their ranks and increasingly his work is rightly regarded as incompatible with revolution, particularly since that term is now expanded to cover sexual and personal reactions against reaction and reality. However, it is certainly not incompatible with reciprocity, and may be destined to play an important part in unmasking the shallow rationalizations and trivial excuses which are routinely used to justify both revolution and reaction in their many guises. Just as the wide currency given to psychoanalytic ideas during its first and second phases did much to unmask the hypocrises, evasions and dissimulations on which earlier and more tractable psychopathologies such as hysteria were based, so psychoanalysis in its third phase may be able to contribute significantly to revealing the lies and self-deceptions on which anything other than genuine reciprocity is based. In this respect nothing can be more significant than its insights into the true nature of human altruism and nothing more important than its firm foundation in a general theory of altruism such as that suggested here.

It seems that reaction aims to restore traditional, compulsive identifications like those discussed earlier in the case of punitive monotheism. Like the individual obsessional neuroses which such collective identifications resemble, aggressive drives originating in the ID are directed back against the EGO as a sense of guilt and remorse through the internalization of an exacting and punitive SuperEGO. Hence the emphasis on law, order, tradition, collective identification and obsessional forms of religion so common in traditional societies and so appealing to reactionaries of all kinds.

Yet revolution also has its own characteristic psychopathology based, not on the introjection of aggressive drives because of compulsive identification with parental figures, but on the projection of passive demands through a differentiation between 'them', the guilty parents/government/capitalists/Jews or whoever, and 'us', the abused, exploited, misunderstood and generally guiltless children, racial brothers or class sisters. Such psychopathology is paranoid rather than obsessional in form and characteristically given to elaborate delusions, often of persecution by the guilty parties. Hence the protest, criticism and recrimination directed against legitimate authority, the astonishing toleration of all kinds of illegitimate violence, and the concern with disadvantage, exploitation and alleged injustice so typical of the revolutionary mentality.

By no means unrelated to this are the conflicts peculiar to industrial adolescence which can complicate the situation by compromising the process of psychological maturation and individuation on which free societies depend. Their psychological foundation in rational self-interest and robust individualism is weakened if adolescents fail to emancipate themselves from infantile dependency and have difficulty in resolving the conflicts with parental values which such latent dependency betrays. This irrational, unconsciously-motivated desire to differentiate from the parents at any cost implicitly suggests a strategy of unconditional and indiscriminate defection logically – and often actually – similar to revolutionary politics which seeks to establish a social structure based on induced altruism and enforced cooperation rather than one founded on reciprocity and free exchange.

By contrast to the three previous psychologically-fundamental socio-economic revolutions represented by primal hunting and gathering, agriculture and pastoralism, industrialization cannot resolve the inevitable parent–offspring conflicts to which it gives rise by enforcing identifications with parental values either during adolescent initiation or during childhood socialization. On the contrary, the unique crisis represented by industrialization seems to require, not irrational and unconditional cooperation brought about by compulsive kin-altruistic identifications, but uncoerced cooperation based on the genuine individualism and rational self-interest of reciprocal altruism. Whereas the former process of compulsive identification is based psychologically on the installation of the SuperEGO, the latter can only be described as one of the emancipation of the EGO. Whether industrial adolescence can adapt to the demands of these unprecedented requirements remains to be seen, but psychological insight into the problem must be valuable and it may well be here that psychoanalysis is destined to make one of its decisive contributions to the future of free societies.

Throughout its history psychoanalysis has had but one aim: the enlargement, enhancement and emancipation of the individual EGO from exorbitant and irrational compulsions of the SuperEGO and from impulsive and uncomprehending enslavement to the peremptory demands of the ID. In its capacity to provide the EGO with reliable internal insights into itself, its ID and SuperEGO, psychoanalysis is the natural extension and counterpart of the EGO's objective insights into external reality which, in their most highly elaborated form, we call natural science. If my earlier remarks, both about the current plight of psychoanalysis and about the rediscovery of Freud by Darwinists, are to be taken seriously, then an end may be in sight both to the sectarian isolation of psychoanalysis within the psychoanalytic institutes, and to the scientific quarantine of Freud's thinking, which has led to its elaboration by psychoanalysts, but to its almost complete avoidance by just about everyone else. If something like the general theory of altruism proposed here ever came to function as a paradigm for behavioural science then Freud's insights, relinquishing their hitherto almost exclusive therapeutic concern as he himself foresaw, might come to form part of a single unified description of organic nature, one extending from basic principles of evolutionary biology and the biochemistry of the genetic code up to the elaborated details of social and economic systems and the psychology of culture itself.

If this were to come about in a third phase of its development, psychoanalysis would finally achieve the status which its founder always foresaw for it: one alongside the natural sciences, a place for himself as successor to Copernicus and Darwin, the only twentieth-century equal of Einstein. It would also have the effect of placing psychoanalysis in its proper relation to social theory: as the vital but hitherto neglected link between the ultimate biological determinants of behaviour and the observed complexities, contradictions and contrarieties of culture. It would make psychoanalytic insights into the reality of human nature and motivation the natural basis for reciprocity in human interactions and provide a sound, scientific foundation for the inevitable concern with truth and falsehood which such reciprocity entails.

Bibliography

R. D. Alexander, *Darwinism and Human Affairs*, Seattle, 1979.

R. Axelrod, *The Evolution of Cooperation*, New York, 1984.

C. Badcock, *Levi-Strauss*, London, 1975.

—— *The Psychoanalysis of Culture*, Oxford, 1980.

—— *Madness and Modernity*, Oxford, 1983.

D. Barash, *Sociobiology: The Whisperings Within*, New York, 1979.

—— *Sociobiology and Behaviour*, 2nd edn, London, 1982.

J. H. Crook, *The Evolution of Human Consciousness*, Oxford, 1980.

C. Darwin, *The Descent of Man*, London, 1875.

R. Dawkins, *The Extended Phenotype*, Oxford, 1982.

—— 'Twelve Misunderstandings of Kin Selection', *Zeitschrift für Tierpsychologie*, 51, 1979.

R. B. Edgerton, *The Individual in Cultural Adaptation*, Berkley, 1971.

L. Eisely, *Darwin's Century*, Garden City N.Y., 1958.

K. R. Eissler, 'Irreverent Remarks about the Present and Future of Psychoanalysis', *International Journal of Psychoanalysis*, 50, 1969.

E. Evans-Pritchard, *Nuer Religion*, Oxford, 1956.

R. Fox, *The Red Lamp of Incest*, London, 1980.

A. Freud, *The Ego and the Mechanisms of Defence*, London, 1966.

—— *Normality and Pathology in Childhood*, London, 1966.

—— Conversation with Joseph Sandler in *Bulletin of the Hampstead Clinic*, 6, 1983.

—— 'A Study-guide to Freud's Writings', in *Psychoanalytic Psychology of Normal Development*, London, 1982.

S. Freud, *Totem and Taboo*, Standard Edition of the *Complete Psychological Works of Sigmund Freud*, vol. XIII.

—— 'On Narcissism', Standard Edn, XIV.

—— 'Repression', Standard Edn, XIV.

—— 'Mourning and Melancholia', Standard Edn, XIV.

—— *Introductory Lectures on Psychoanalysis*, Standard Edn, XVI.

—— *Group Psychology and the Analysis of the Ego*, Standard Edn, XVIII.

—— *Preface to Aichorn's Wayward Youth*, Standard Edn, XIX.

—— 'The Economic Problem of Masochism', Standard Edn, XIX.

—— *New Introductory Lectures on Psychoanalysis*, Standard Edn, XXII.

—— 'Analysis Terminable and Interminable', Standard Edn, XXIII.

M. and R. Friedman, *Free to Choose*, Harmondsworth, 1980.

—— *The Tyranny of the Status Quo*, Harmondsworth, 1985.

J. Hajnal, 'Two Kinds of Pre-industrial Household Formation', in R. Wall, J. Robin and P. Laslett (eds), *Family Forms in Historic Europe*, Cambridge, 1983.

W. D. Hamilton, 'Innate Social Aptitudes of Man: An Approach from Evolutionary Genetics', in R. Fox (ed.), *Biosocial Anthropology*, London, 1975.

F. A. Hayek, *Law, Legislation and Liberty*, London, 1983.

S. J. Heims, *John Neumann and Norbert Wiener*, Cambridge, Mass., 1981.

R. J. Hollingdale (ed.), *A Nietzsche Reader*, Harmondsworth, 1977.

K. Hopkins, 'Brother–Sister Marriage in Roman Egypt', *Comparative Studies in Society and History*, 22, 1980.

D. Hull, *Darwin and His Critics*, Cambridge, Mass., 1973.

J. Imperato-McGinley et al., 'Androgens and the Evolution of Male-gender Identity among Male Pseudohermaphrodites with a 5α-reductase Deficiency', *The New England Journal of Medicine*, 300, no.22, 1979.

C. Jolly, 'The Seed-Eaters: A New Model of Hominid Differentiation Based on a Baboon Analogy', *Man*, 5, 1970.

E. Jones, *The Life and Work of Sigmund Freud*, London, 1953-7.

W. Kaufmann, *Discovering the Mind*, vol. III, *Freud versus Adler and Jung*, New York, 1980.

N. Kretchmer, 'Lactose and Lactase', *Scientific American*, 227, 1972.

T. S. Kuhn, *The Copernican Revolution*, Cambridge, Mass., 1957.

—— *The Structure of Scientific Revolutions*, Chicago, 1970.

C. Lévi-Strauss, *The Elementary Structures of Kinship*, Boston, 1969.

G. Lienhardt, *Divinity and Experience*, Oxford, 1961.

H. and Y. Lowenfeld, 'Our Permissive Society and the Superego', *The Psychoanalytic Quarterly*, 39, 1970.

C. J. Lumsden and E. O. Wilson, *Promethean Fire*, Cambridge, Mass., 1983.

D. McKnight, *Australian Aborigine Marriage-class Systems* (in press).

N. J. Marks, *Science and the Making of the Modern World*, London, 1983.

B. Martin, *A Sociology of Contemporary Change*, Oxford, 1981.

M. Olson, *The Logic of Collective Action*, Cambridge, Mass., 1965.

—— *The Rise and Decline of Nations*, New Haven, 1982.

L. Ritvo, 'Darwin as the Origin of Freud's Neo-Lamarckianism', *Journal of the American Psychoanalytic Association*, 13, 1965.

G. Roheim, 'Psychoanalysis of Primitive Cultural Types', *International Journal of Psychoanalysis*, 23, 1932.

—— *The Riddle of the Sphinx*, London, 1934.

—— 'The Primal Horde and Incest in Central Australia', *Journal of Criminal Psychopathology*, 3, 1942.

—— *The Origin and Function of Culture*, New York, 1943.

—— *Children of the Desert*, New York, 1974.

M. Ruse and E. O. Wilson, 'The Evolution of Ethics', *New Scientist*, 17 Oct. 1985.

J. Shepher, *Incest: A Biosocial View*, New York, 1983.

P. Singer, *The Expanding Circle*, Oxford, 1981.

A. Smith, *The Wealth of Nations*, Harmondsworth, 1980.

M. E. Spiro, *Oedipus in the Trobriands*, Chicago, 1982.

L. Stone, *The Family, Sex and Marriage in England, 1500-1800*, Harmondsworth, 1977.

R. Trivers, 'The Evolution of Reciprocal Altruism', *Quarterly Review of Biology*, 46, 1971.

—— 'Parental Investment and Sexual Selection', in B. Campbell (ed.), *Sexual Selection and the Descent of Man*, Chicago, 1972.

—— 'Parent–Offspring Conflict', *American Zoologist*, 14, 1974.

—— 'Sociobiology and Politics' in E. White (ed.), *Sociobiology and Human Politics*, Lexington and Toronto, 1981.

—— *Social Evolution*, Menlo Park, 1985.

R. Trivers and D. Willard, 'Natural Selection of Parental Ability to Vary the Sex Ratio of Offspring', *Science*, 179, 1973.

P. van den Berghe, *Human Family Systems*, New York, 1979.

M. de Vries, 'The Problem of Infanticide: A Reinterpretation of the Post-partum Attachment Period', in K. Immelmann et al. (eds), *Behavioural Development: the Bielfeld Interdisciplinary Project*, Cambridge, 1979.

E. O. Wilson, *Sociobiology*, Cambridge, Mass., 1975.

J. Woodburn, 'Hunters and Gatherers Today and Reconstruction of the Past', in E. Gellner (ed.), *Soviet and Western Anthropology*, London, 1980.

D. Wrong, 'The Over-socialized Conception of Man in Modern Sociology', *The American Sociological Review*, XXVI, 1961.

Index